ELFEGO BACA
DESTINED to SURVIVE

by Robert J. Alvarado

Other Works

by Robert J. Alvarado
www.youngpistolero.com

Award Winning Young Pistolero Series
The saga of Rafael Ortega de Estrada, a young Mexican peón on the run riding a stolen Appaloosa stallion after shooting the haciendero who raped his younger sister. Heading north, Rafael enters the United States in 1866 to find life on the other side of the border holds new dangers along with the promise of a new life. This gritty tale is set in the American Southwest as Americans and Mexicans struggle after the Mexican-American War.

Young Pistolero (Book 1) 2013 Sierra Press
    2018 Finalist for Drama TV Series category, by the Latino Books into Movies Awards by Latino Literacy Now

    #1 Fiction Book for 2015; by The Latino Author, by Corina Martinez Chaudhry

Star of the Young Pistolero (Book 2) 2014 Sierra Press

Death Stalks the Young Pistolero (Book 3) 2015 Sierra Press
    #1 Fiction Book for 2016; by The Latino Author

Legacy for the Young Pistolero (Book 4) 2017 Sierra Press
    #3 Fiction Book for 2017; by The Latino Author

A Reckoning for the Young Pistolero (Book 5) 2018 Sierra Press

Young Pistolero Series (con't)
Dangerous Venture (Book 6) 2019 Sierra Press
Justified Vengeance (Book 7) 2019 Sierra Press
The Black Phantom (Book 8) 2020 Sierra Press

Fiction
The Jalapeño Republic 2020 Sierra Press
    2021 International Latino Book Award Medalist. Insights from the ILBA judges, "It was an interesting book, quite different from most futuristic novels I have read."

Jake Flores Mysterys
Just Vanished –2020 Sierra Press
    2021 International Latino Book Award Medalist. Insights from the ILBA judges, "From the moment you start reading it, you imagine an action TV series that keeps you involved."

Zia Westerns
Set in the New Mexico and Arizona territories of the Southwest, these westerns draw from the Southwest's unique flavor. Originally part of New Spain and then Mexico, the Spanish settlers and native Indians forged an informal peace until the years after the Mexican-American War brought them into the Wild West. These stories are set during this chaotic time and attempt to paint a realistic picture of the meaning of the Zia symbol.

    The Spanish Sword 2020 Sierra Press
    2021 International Latino Book Award Medalist. Insights from the ILBA judges, "This book is carefully crafted and felt thoroughly researched."

Praises and Awards

"Bob Alvarado's "Elfego Baca, Destined to Survive" is a most welcome addition to the lore of this famous New Mexican lawman. From Disney movie hero of the 50's to the many books written about him, Baca continues to be one of the most well known heroes in the Wild West of New Mexico. Only Billy the Kid garners more attention than Baca. I've been reading books about Elfego Baca, you might say following the trail of Baca, since I was a kid, and this is one I keep going back to time and again."
  Rudolfo Anaya...acclaimed novelist, poet,
  playwright, professor emeritus, 2015 National
  Humanities Medal Award recipient

"The author does a fantastic job of providing the reader with enough historical background of how the state of Texas and New Mexico became part of the United States and also detailing with the atmosphere of prejudice and biases against people of color during that time — especially for Mexican and Spanish U.S. citizens. In addition, he does a magnificent job of providing the reader with a chronological history of how the Spaniards conquered the Americas (Cortez and other explorers of that time). This gives insight into Elfego Baca's ancestral lineage to the Vaca/Baca clan and possibly to his bravery and risk taking. In this history book, the author further details some of the Spaniard practices such as the importance of baptismal priests and the corruption that existed within this practice, as well as the bigotries amongst the Spaniard's own society; Peninsulares versus Criollos versus Mestizos and how these inequalities possibly carried on over to new generations.

This is the true story of a brave man named Elfego Baca whose gunfight should have gone down in the history books as one of the greats of all time, even surpassing that of the O.K. Corral fight involving Wyatt Earp, his brothers, and Doc Holiday against the Clanton and McLaury Brothers.

Elfego Baca singlehandedly fought and avoided being shot during this 4,000-bullet gun battle against 80 Texas cowboys using only a small shack for shelter. So why hasn't much been written in the history books about this courageous man who sought to stop the injustice during the late 1880s? If truth be told, it is most likely because he was considered a "Mexican" and his story was not considered important by mainstream America.

The author's intent was to provide both a historical perspective, but yet to give insight into this one man's life who was very much a part of American history. The photographs included, also provide the reader with a good perspective on life during the time of Elfego Baca."

by Corina Martinez Chaudhry
...CEO, TheLatinoAuthor.com

ELFEGO BACA
DESTINED to SURVIVE

Copyright 2016 by Robert J. Alvarado
All Rights Reserved.

Printed in the United State of America

IBSN-13: 978-0991477739

Published by Sierra Press
First Printing, July 2016

Cover art and design by John Flinn
Graphic art by Daniel David Alvarado

Disclaimer

This book is a work of investigational history where the names of characters, places, and events are the product of the author's collective research on the topic from historical documents, books, and personal contacts. Although the author and publisher have made every effort to ensure the historical information in this book is fundamentally correct, the author and publisher do not assume and hereby disclaim any liability to any party for any loss, damage, or disruption caused by errors or omissions, whether such errors or omissions result from negligence, accident, or any other cause.

Some material in this book may contain graphic content and language to accurately depict the events of history.

Without limiting the rights under copyright reserved above, no part of this publication may be reproduced, stored in or introduced into a retrieval system, or transmitted, in any form, or by any means (electronic, mechanical, photocopying, recording, or otherwise), without the prior written permission of the copyright owner, except by a reviewer or researcher who may quote brief passages.

Published by Sierra Press, June 2016
Website: www.youngpistolero.com

Dedication

. . . for the memory of Elfego Baca.

Table of Contents

Acknowledgements 11
The Castration 13
Who Was Elfego Baca? 23
Spain Inadvertently Discovers a New World 31
Spanish Conquest of the Aztec Empire 37
Life in New Spain 49
Searching for the Seven Cities of Gold 53
A New Nation — Mexico 73
The Texas Rebellion 79
New Mexico Territory 101
San Francisco Valley, New Mexico, Territory 107
The Slaughters 127
Baca New Mexico Origins 135
Young Elfego 151
Trouble in Socorro 165
Blood Will Be Spilled 179
Elfego Stands Tall 197
Life in Socorro 207
Deputy Elfego Baca Arrives 219
Mexicans on the Warpath 229
Four-thousand Bullets 239
Elfego's Lasting Mark on Frisco 257
Elfego Tried for Murder 267
Life after Frisco 273
Conclusion 289
Bibliography and Sources 291
Notes 303

Acknowledgements

The most fantastic treasures I found during my research were these two *caballeros* — Gilbert Eugene Baca and Henry Martinez.

Gilbert Baca is the grandnephew of Elfego Baca. Gilbert knew his granduncle personally before Elfego died in 1945. He told me the man, he knew as his granduncle Elfego, was in many ways larger-than-life. Gil Baca lives in Rio Rancho, New Mexico, and is retired from the Postal Service. He and his wife Bonnie have collected all known books and articles on Elfego and were most helpful with the Baca genealogy and history on the Baca family. He has continued to be a wealth of personal information and encouragement on this project. He graciously shared any and all documents and information, which has been most helpful, and I owe him many thanks.

Henry Martinez is the great-grandson of Epitacio Martinez. His great-grandfather was shot while trying to keep the Texas cowboys from harming *el Burro,* the incident that brought Elfego Baca to Frisco Plaza in 1884. His great-grandfather was tied to a post and used for target practice by the Texas cowboys. Upper Frisco Plaza was later renamed Reserve and is now the county seat of Catron County, New Mexico. Henry Martinez currently lives in Reserve and has a store called Henry's Corner. He was very helpful with information about his ancestors and general knowledge of the area.

Henry and Gil started *The Elfego Baca Project* in 2001 to promote Elfego Baca's story and to bring awareness of his life and legend. Through this non-profit organization, they have purchased land with funds provided by the New Mexico State Legislature for a memorial park. The organization also commissioned James

N. Muir to create a statue of Elfego Baca, which stands at the location of the shootout in the heart of the village of Reserve, New Mexico, and they are working with the State of New Mexico to obtain historical markers.

I would like to thank Daniel David Alvarado of Adobe Images, Phoenix, Arizona, for the cover design and for formatting the illustrations and pictures.

My wife, Ellen, deserves both my love and appreciation for her countless hours of researching, reading, critiquing, her support on this project, and in so many other ways. Thank you my darling.

I owe a debt of gratitude to the previous biographers whose insightful books were an inspiration. I hope my effort to document the history and genealogy of Elfego completes the circle they started. Their books should be an interesting read for anyone wanting to know the rest of the story.

My thanks to the Socorro County Historical Society for providing many pictures of Socorro from the mid to late 1800s. Judge Robert T. Baca, Mary Baca Aguilar, and Gil Baca provided family pictures never previously published. Henry Martinez provided the history and photographs of his family's settlement of the San Francisco valley, now called Reserve, New Mexico.

In general, like all historical biographers I am indebted to all the libraries, universities, Catholic genealogy records, historical collections, and individuals who maintain historical information, which makes writing this type of work possible.

The Castration

Woodstove smoke, along with the aroma of freshly toasted tortillas, permeated the San Francisco valley on a cool late afternoon in the Upper Frisco Plaza. It was mid-October of 1884 and colors on the surrounding hills hinted of the upcoming winter to this beautiful part of western Socorro County, in the New Mexico Territory. Epitacio Martinez was on his way home tasting the air, which only made his empty stomach growl more. He left his home in Middle Frisco Plaza early this morning working his way up the San Francisco River valley, past Upper Frisco, in search of a work horse which he sorely needed. His day was long and tiresome and he had no luck finding a work horse for sale. Now, the smells in the plaza peaked his hunger to be on his way home.

Approaching Upper Frisco Plaza from the north, Epitacio hurried his horse along the main path wanting to keep his course from crossing in front of Milligan's liquor emporium, if the Texas cowboys were about. Before he got there he heard familiar gunfire. It was enough for him to know the Texas cowboys from the Slaughter Cattle Ranch were having rounds of cheap whiskey at Milligans. Bill Milligan happily overcharged the local cowboys for cheap, watered-down whiskey, regardless of the usual consequences. The more whiskey the cowboys drank the more trouble it meant for any non-Texans, especially those of Spanish descent. Just weeks ago the Texas cowboys roped a *señorita* and she had not been seen again. Epitacio wanted no part of any trouble with the Texans — not today or any day. He could see the front of the saloon down the street and got ready to spur his horse into a gallop to pass it before any of the Texans spotted him, but there was already a commotion in the street.

"*¡Burro, quédate aquí!*" he heard Deputy Pedro Sarracino yell at a young Hispanic man, nicknamed *Burro,* to stay with him and not to run. Everyone called the man *el Burro,* because he was considered a dunce or 'dumb like a donkey.' *Burro* didn't listen to the deputy and continued running down the plaza past Milligans yelling he had to get home for dinner. The deputy shouted at *Burro* to stop, but the young man ignored the pleas. It was only seconds before the Texas cowboys spotted him. They stopped shooting at Milligan's ceiling and turned their drunken attention toward the running Mexican.

"Yeeee ha! Lookee here boys we got r'seves a stray doggie," one of the seven cowboys yelled out.

"Go git that stray, Len," another one shouted.

Running out of Milligan's, Len jumped onto his horse on a run, Texas style. Once aboard, he grabbed his rope and twirled a loop above his head. Twirling it twice he threw the loop at *Burro's* feet. Len was the best Slaughter steer-dogger and caught the two legged 'doggie' with the first throw. As soon as he pulled the rope tight toppling *el Burro,* his cattle trained horse came to a habitual dusty halt. Seeing his prey was securely roped, he turned his horse around and dragged the man back to Milligans, where the rest of the cowboys were shooting up in the air and hollering.

El Burro was dusty from head to toe, lying on the street and spitting dirt. Every time *Burro* tried to untie his legs and get up, Len yanked tightly on the rope knocking him back down to the dusty street.

"Len! Ya ain't dun with that doggie yet. First ya catch 'em, then ya gotta cut 'em," hollered out one of the laughing Texans.

"I cain't do it! I only catch 'em for Butch. That's his job!" Len hollered back.

"Hey Butch, we got us a doggie fer ya!" one of the cowboys yelled into the saloon.

Watching what they were doing to poor *Burro*, Deputy Sarracino screamed, *"¡Estop!"* in broken English at the cowboys and headed toward them drawing for his gun. Shaking, the frightened deputy couldn't get his gun out of the holster quickly enough. Two of the Texans had their guns drawn and pointed at him. Sarracino put up his hands waiting for bullets that would surely kill him, as he was certain these cowboys would shoot him without a thought.

Sarracino was backing away from the Texans when he saw Epitacio Martinez run down the street to where *el Burro* was struggling with the ropes around his legs. Epitacio got down on his knees and untied him and helped him up.

"¡Hijos de putas!" Martinez cursed at the Texans calling them 'sons of whores.' The Slaughter cowboys stopped and were taken back a bit by the bravery of the Mexican man freeing their 'doggie.' Normally, Mexicans hid from the cowboys and never stood up to them without dire consequences.

"You stinkn' Mex," Butch yelled a typical retort back at Epitacio, not knowing what the Spanish curse meant.

"Let's git 'im boys," one of the other Texans yelled out.

Len grabbed *Burro* and two others caught Epitacio. One held Epitacio by the neck and the other by the legs. Picking him up they tied him with ropes to a nearby fence post, then they went back to where Len and Butch held *Burro*.

"OK boys, git that doggie up on Milligan's counter," Butch said. Len and one of the other cowboys grabbed *Burro* and lifted him high. Inside Milligans they flopped him onto the bar counter. Epitacio and Deputy Sarracino could hear him screaming for the cowboys to stop. The deputy looked at Epitacio tied to the post and heard *Burro's* screams from inside Milligans, but did nothing to stop it. Though armed, he stood paralyzed with fear.

Butch pulled out a castrating knife from a leather pouch he always carried on his belt. He was called Butch because he was 'The Butcher,' the best of the castrators at the Slaughter Cattle Ranch.

The Slaughter cowboys held the screaming *Burro* down on the counter; one of the Texans sat on his chest and arms and two others held his legs. Butch wasted no time pulling at *Burro's pantalones*. He grabbed *Burro's* testicles with his left hand and with a single swipe cut them off. Butch held them up and all the cowboys hooted and hollered. Walking to the door of the saloon, he grinned before throwing them at Deputy Pedro Sarracino.

"No little greaser's for this one," Butch growled. *El Burro's* testicles fell into the dirt in front of the stunned and helpless deputy.

"*¡Cabrones!*" Epitacio yelled out. He called the Texans a derogatory Spanish curse meaning 'he-goats' or men who would allow other men to fornicate with their wives or girl friends.

Butch and the cowboys looked over at the young Mexican tied to the fence post. Epitacio's eyes burned with hatred for the Texans. He squirmed against the tight ropes that bound him to the post.

Butch walked over to where Epitacio was tied and back-handed him across the face. Butch's breath stank of whiskey and his hand was bloody. He paced back about twenty paces to the front of Milligan's store, where the other cowboys were passing a bottle of whiskey around.

"Silver dollar says I can hit the first button on that greaser," Butch bragged and pointed at Epitacio. He took aim at the top button of Epitacio's coat.

Butch missed the button but not Epitacio. The bullet hit him on the right shoulder. Butch lost two bucks. Three other cowboys took their turn and lost money trying to shoot the buttons from Epitacio's coat. The Texas cowboys finally lost interest in their game, perhaps thinking they had killed the young Mexican who slumped on the post. They mounted their horses and galloped off, shooting at stray dogs and chickens as they headed back to the Slaughter Cattle Ranch.

* * *

The preceding is a dramatization of a gruesome incident which actually happened in October 1884 at a place called Upper Frisco Plaza, in Socorro County of the New Mexico Territory of the United States of America. Epitacio Martinez was hit four times, but amazingly survived the shooting, living the rest of his life in the San Francisco valley. The real name of the man called *Burro* and his legacy has been lost to history.

* * *

Upper Frisco Plaza is now the town of Reserve, New Mexico in Catron County. High in the mountains, the sleepy town belies the amazing incident of 1884. I became intrigued with Elfego's story and traveled to Reserve looking for truth in the legend. What I found has become an amazing personal journey and an amazing story of one man's life and how fate brought him to this troubled spot and almost took his life, but destiny had other plans.

My research started in Reserve where I met with Henry Martinez, great-grandson of Epitacio Martinez. He took me to the center of a dusty lot where a statue of Elfego defending himself against the Texans stands. The buildings of the old Upper Frisco Plaza are long gone, as are the cattle and the Texas cowboys, but somehow standing next to Elfego's statue you can imagine the guns blazing.

Memorial statue of Elfego Baca by James N. Muir, located in the village of Reserve, New Mexico. Photograph taken by the author, 2012. This memorial was constructed under the leadership of Henry Martinez by the Elfego Baca Project, Inc. and Catron County, with a grant from the State of New Mexico, to commemorate the life, honor, and bravery of Elfego Baca.

Close-up of the memorial plaque of Elfego Baca by James N. Muir, located in the village of Reserve, New Mexico. Photograph taken by the author, 2012.

The plaque reads:

ELFEGO BACA 1865 – 1945

In October 1884, seven drunken cowboys committed horrific acts against two Mexican men in Upper Frisco, (modern day Reserve). Just a stone throw from where you now stand, in Milligan's Saloon, a man known as El Burro was brutally tortured and Epitacio Martinez, coming to the aid of his friend, was bound and shot for target practice. Both men lived. The Frisco deputy sheriff, Pedro Sarracino, outnumbered and overwhelmed, rode to Socorro for help. Nineteen-year-old deputy Elfego

Destined to Survive

Baca rode back to Frisco with Sarracino intent on seeking justice.

Three days later, Baca observed one cowboy butting another on the head and firing several rounds with his pistol. Justice of the Peace Lopez stood by helplessly, saying the Slaughter outfit had 150 cowboys on their payroll and could not be stopped. Determined and fearless, Baca promptly arrested the cowboy. A large group of cowboys gathered and demanded his release. Baca shot into the group wounding one man and they dispersed. But the following day, 80 enraged ranch hands rode into the town intent on freeing the arrested cowboy and avenging the indignity of his arrest. A trial was held and the cowboy was released. Baca, sensing a gunfight, retreated to a jacal belonging to Geronimo Armijo and barricaded himself inside. Baca kept his six-shooter blazing for 36 hours, pausing just long enough to cook some tortillas and beef stew. Protected by mud and picket walls, a sunken dirt floor, and an icon of Nuestra Senora Santa Anna, Baca braved dynamite and some 4,000 rounds of gunfire shot in his direction by the Texas cowboys.

On the third day Baca agreed to give himself up to Deputy Rose from Socorro but refused to turn over his guns. Baca, unscathed throughout the gunfight, had killed two cowboys and wounded two more.

The atrocities stopped.

"I WILL SHOW THE TEXANS THERE IS AT LEAST ONE MEXICAN IN THE COUNTY WHO IS NOT AFRAID OF AN AMERICAN COWBOY"
ELFEGO BACA – 1884

Who Was Elfego Baca?

The first task on my research list for writing this biography of Elfego Baca was to do an internet Google search on "famous gunfights of the old west." From the resulting list I followed and read the many links to articles of famous gunfighters and gunfights. It took quite a lot of digging before I found any reference to Elfego's gunfight with eighty Texas cowboys in 1884 at Upper Frisco Plaza.

I then changed the Google search criteria to "gunfights of the old west" taking the word 'famous' out of the search criteria. With this search I did find a reference to Elfego and the Frisco Shootout quicker, but still after a bit of digging. Next I navigated to Wikipedia, the free online encyclopedia, and did a search on "list of old west gunfights." Paging down the list there was an entry titled, "Frisco Shootout, Elfego Baca December 1, 1884, Reserve, New Mexico." The Frisco Shootout, as it was called, actually happened in late October of 1884.

Well, at least I was finding some references as a starting point. I followed the Wikipedia link to its site and found this short synopsis of the shootout between Elfego and eighty Texas cowboys:

> The Frisco Shootout was an Old West gunfight that occurred on December 1, 1884, involving lawman Elfego Baca. The shootout happened in Reserve, New Mexico, and stemmed from Baca's arrest of a cowboy who had been shooting into the air and into buildings at random while intoxicated.

Shortly after the arrest was made, Baca was confronted by a large number of the cowboy's friends. Baca took refuge in the house of local resident Geronimo Armijo. A standoff ensued, during which the cowboys increased in number to around eighty men. Legend has it that the cowboys fired more than 4,000 rounds into the house, but there is little way of confirming just how many rounds were fired exactly. Baca was not wounded by any of the rounds fired, but did return fire killing four of the cowboys, and wounding eight others. The standoff ended when the cowboys were unable to acquire more ammunition. With their ammunition supply depleted, they simply withdrew. The fight had lasted thirty six hours.

The cowboy that had been originally arrested by Baca served his time in jail for disturbing the peace and drunkenness, and was released. The cowboys pursued Baca through legal means, attempting to have him imprisoned for the killing of their four comrades. In May, 1885, Baca was indicted for the killing of one of the men.

However, when the door of Geronimo Armijo's house was introduced as evidence, having over four hundred bullet holes in it, Baca was acquitted.

Baca went on to become a licensed attorney and a Deputy US Marshal.[1]

In this synopsis and from other websites it was stated Elfego had taken refuge in Geronimo Armijo's house, in reality a *jacal,* which was basically a stick and mud hut. This building was hardly a fortress for young Elfego against eighty armed men. For thirty-six hours the cowboys pumped four thousand rounds into the *jacal* hoping to kill Elfego. Most versions of the story indicate the cowboys ran out of ammunition, though not exactly true. After a negotiated truce, Elfego came out of the *jacal* unharmed. Additionally, the typical story on most websites, including Wikipedia, credits Elfego of killing four Texans and wounding another eight. The actual fatality count — Elfego killed two Texans and wounded another two.

I pondered why the Frisco Shootout was not the most famous gunfight of the old west. Undoubtedly the most famous of all American gunfights is the gunfight at the O.K. Corral in Tombstone, Arizona. Wyatt Earp and his brothers, Morgan and Virgil, along with Doc Holliday, went up against the Clanton brothers and the McLaury brothers. The odds in the beginning of the confrontation were four against four, however, Ike Clanton ran away before the shooting began. The gunfight at the O.K. Corral is documented as about a thirty-second gunfight which took place around 3:00 p.m. on Wednesday, October 26, 1881. Less than thirty shots are thought to have been fired during the gunfight. The two McLaury brothers and Billy Clanton died at the scene. Doc Holliday and Wyatt's two brothers were wounded.

Now compare thirty seconds and less than thirty rounds fired with essentially even odds, four against four at the O.K. Corral, to one Elfego Baca against eighty

Texas cowboys shooting approximately four thousand rounds. Although the O.K. Corral shootout occurred on open ground, Elfego's only protection was a mud shack and a Catholic statue of Saint Anne. After thirty-six hours of firing, Elfego came out alive and unscathed.

By far Elfego's Frisco Shootout was the longest and largest of any on record. Typically, old west gunfights were between only two people, such as the Bill Hickok versus David Tutt shootout in July of 1865. Most were over swiftly with one of the participants lying dead. In the Las Vegas Saloon shootout in Las Vegas, New Mexico, on January 22, 1880, four rough-housing cowboys met up against two lawmen. Marshal Joe Carson was killed along with at least one of the cowboys.

Why then is the Frisco Shootout not the most famous of the old west gunfights? Is it because Elfego was of Spanish descent? After all Elfego Baca was an American who lived in Socorro, New Mexico. The gunfight took place on American soil, although New Mexico and Arizona were territories at the time and not yet states.

Additional searching of the gunfights of the old west brought another interesting issue to my attention. Only a few listed gunfights or gunfighters had Spanish surnames. The other listed Spanish-named gunfighters were outlaws, not lawmen and usually on the wrong end of a bullet. It should be noted there is a Wikipedia listing for Mariano Barela (18?? – 188?) Sheriff and U.S. Marshal in Mesilla, New Mexico. Unfortunately, no links are provided and his history is not available.

In the aftermath of the Mexican-American War of 1846 – 1848, whereby the United States obtained the northern territories of Mexico, the population of New Mexico was primarily of Spanish descent. Below is Article Nine of the Treaty of Guadalupe Hidalgo drafted after the

Mexican-American War in 1848, stating that any person living in the territories became a United States citizen:

> ARTICLE IX
> The Mexicans who, in the territories aforesaid, shall not preserve the character of citizens of the Mexican Republic, conformably with what is stipulated in the preceding article, shall be incorporated into the Union of the United States, and be admitted at the proper time (to be judged of by the Congress of the United States) to the enjoyment of all the rights of citizens of the United States, according to the principles of the Constitution; and in the meantime, shall be maintained and protected in the free enjoyment of their liberty and property, and secured in the free exercise of their religion without restriction.

The law gave Mexicans living in the territories the rights and freedoms enjoyed by all citizens of the United States, but in practice there was a wide divide in culture and acceptance. Evident in my research, much of the literature written about the territories at this time, citizens of Hispanic descent are always referred to as Mexicans or 'greasers' or other derogatory names, and not Americans. In many books and newspaper articles from the time, the term Americans was reserved to mean white or Anglo-Americans. Even today in the twenty-first century most any citizen of any Hispanic descent is generically called Mexican.

Author's Note: In this book persons born or living in the United States or its territories will be referred to as Hispanics, in reference to Spanish-Americans or Mexican-Americans. An exception to this is the use of Mexican by reference materials and when used in narrative from the Anglo-American point of view during the time period of this book.

Unlike many of the other gunfights of the old west, the Frisco Shootout was heroically won by a Hispanic American. Newspapers and writers of the time may not have been comfortable expounding on this unlikely hero.

By the 1950s some things had changed. As the television era became readily available, Walt Disney began releasing a made-for-television series called Walt Disney's "Wonderful World of Color." One series was on Elfego Baca.

In 1958 Walt Disney Studios released a television miniseries entitled "The Nine Lives of Elfego Baca" starring Robert Loggia in the title role. Significant was the care Disney took to depict the famous siege in as authentic a manner as possible, given the known details. Among those who appeared in the series were Skip Homeier, Raymond Bailey, and I. Stanford Jolley. Disney produced ten episodes of "The Nine Lives of Elfego Baca" during the 1958 and 1959 TV seasons. Episodes of the series were later edited into a movie titled "Elfego Baca: Six Gun Law" which was released in 1962.

To facilitate my research, Gil Baca allowed me to borrow an original copy of Elfego's autobiography:

Elfego Baca's —
    Here Comes Elfego! The Autobiography of Elfego Baca

This small hand-printed book from 1924 with limited circulation is a collector's item.

My web surfing also found links to an autobiography and several biographies on Elfego Baca which have already been written including the following:

Kyle Crichton's —
    Law and Order, Ltd. The Rousing Life of Elfego Baca of New Mexico

Larry Ball's —
    Elfego Baca in Life and Legend

Howard Bryan's —
    Incredible Elfego Baca Good Man, Bad Man of the Old West

Stan Sager's —
¡Viva Elfego! The Case for Elfego Baca, Hispanic Hero

These biographies go into great detail on Elfego's life during the events of 1884 and after the Frisco Shootout, his political and law careers up to his natural death on August 27, 1945, at his home in Albuquerque, New Mexico. None of the above biographies have an in-depth history of Elfego Baca's long and distinct genealogy, his DNA — the life blood of centuries that flowed through him.

My efforts in writing this biography will focus on his genealogy and the history that brought the Spaniards and Texans to Upper Frisco Plaza in 1884. It will explore Elfego's life before the gunfight, the events leading up to the shootout, his confrontation with the Texans in the San Francisco valley, and his arrest and trial for murder of the Texans who tried to kill him.

My intent is to try to answer the following questions. What shaped a nineteen-year-old young man to take it upon himself to confront the Texans, who were harassing the Hispanic villagers in the San Francisco valley? Where did this kind of bravery originate? Why did Elfego follow this path? Why is the Frisco Shootout not considered the greatest gunfight of the old west?

Many events led up to the five days in October of 1884 where one lone man stood up to eighty Texans. Charting these events which intertwine, asks another question: Was Elfego destined to go to Frisco Plaza and confront the Texans and was he destined to survive?

Spain Inadvertently Discovers a New World

In order to understand the man, Elfego Baca and the events of that fateful October in 1884, one needs to understand how history brought him to the small village in New Mexico to engage in an uncommon act of valor. Was it a random event, an impulsive act, or some deeply rooted innate part of human nature passed along in his DNA for generations?

Elfego's story begins in Spain during the time of the Moorish occupation when the Spaniards rose up as a nation, expelled the Moors, sailed uncharted seas, and discovered America. Elfego's ancestry can be directly traced to those Spaniards who bravely came across the world during the conquest of the Aztec empire. By any standard, the trip across the ocean was at best arduous. Landing in the Americas, or New Spain, was dangerous and life hardly in keeping with glamorous Spain — but they came; they endured; they prospered; they survived! Eventually the descendants of these early settlers, along with Elfego's ancestors, made their way to New Mexico where Elfego was born.

For centuries after the Moors (Muslims) invaded the Iberian Peninsula the call to duty was a Spanish necessity. It was a deep-rooted characteristic of the culture that permeated their lives. The Spanish citizenry would drop their plows, close their shops, leave their classrooms to pick up arms and go to battle against the Moors. To understand the nature of a people who would endure these hardships, the starting point is a basic history of the Spanish exploration and conquest of the Americas by courageous and adventurous Spaniards.

The Moors, crossing the Strait of Gibraltar from North Africa's region called Al-Andalus, conquered Spain and Portugal around 711 AD and held power over the Iberian Peninsula for 780 years. After a progression of battles the Moors held most of the southern parts of Spain, also known as *Moorish Iberia*. They brought their religion, Islam, their language, Arabic, and their architecture of detailed Arabic arches and intricate patterns which can be seen all over southern Spain today. Conquest for control over land mass, resources, and peoples is as old as time, and Spain had endured its share of conquest by the Romans, Visigoths, and Byzantines prior to the Moors.

During this occupation of Spain, battles and skirmishes continued between the Spaniards and the Moors for centuries. One Spanish knight named El Cid Campeador, the Champion, or El Cid, born Rodrigo Diaz de Vivar in 1043, is considered a national Spanish hero who spent most of his life battling the Moors. However, it would not be for four more centuries before the Moors were expelled from the Iberian Peninsula.

The Spaniards battled the Moors through generations of families until the Emirate of Granada surrendered to Ferdinand II and Isabella I, the King and Queen of Spain, on January 2, 1492. Granada was the last Muslim Kingdom on the Iberian Peninsula and this marked the final expulsion of the Moors from Spain.

One might think the cost and effort to expel the Moors from Spain, after centuries of occupation, would have led to a period of peace and tranquility, but the year 1492 is a date most children educated in the United States learn in elementary school. The Spaniards were seeking new worlds, new trade routes, and new riches. The time for exploration had come.

In that year King Ferdinand II and Queen Isabella I commissioned Cristóbal Colón, Christopher Columbus, to discover a westward passage to the Orient to open new trade routes. On the evening of August 3, 1492, Colón set sail from Spain looking for this westward route. Colón captained the flag ship Santa Maria with his other captains on La Niña and La Pinta. On October 12, 1492, they landed at an island we now call the Bahamas. He named it San Salvador, meaning Blessed Saviour, and claimed it for Spain.

Columbus referred to the resident peoples he encountered there as 'Indians' in the mistaken belief he had reached the Indian Ocean. Although Columbus' mistake was soon recognized, the name stuck and for centuries the native people of the Americas were collectively called Indians. This misnomer was perpetuated in naming the surrounding islands. The islands of the Caribbean were named and are still known as the West Indies.

In a personal letter prefacing his hand-written journal, which details his first voyage, Cristóbal Colón vividly evokes his own hopes and binds them all together with the conquest of the infidel, the victory of Christianity, and the westward route to discovery and Christian alliance:

> . . . and I saw the Moorish king come out of the gates of the city and kiss the royal hands of Your Highnesses and of the Prince my Lord; . . . and Your Highnesses, as Catholic Christians and Princes, lovers and promoters of the Holy Christian Faith, and enemies of the false doctrine of Mahomet [sic] and of all idolatries and heresies, you thought of sending me, Cristobal Colon, to the said regions of India to see the said princes and the peoples and the lands, and the characteristics of the lands and of everything and to see how their

conversion to our Holy Faith might be undertaken. And you commanded that I should not go to the East by land, by which way it is customary to go, but by the route to the West, by which route we do not know certain that anyone previously has passed . . . Your Highnesses commanded me to go, with a suitable fleet, to the said regions of India. And for that you granted me great favors and ennobled me so that from then on I might call myself "Don" and would be Grand Admiral of the Ocean Sea and Viceroy and perpetual Governor of all the islands and lands that I might discover and gain and from now on might be discovered and gained in the Ocean Sea; and likewise my eldest son would succeed me and his son him, from generation to generation forever.[2]

Visualize the courage of these men on a voyage to the unknown over treacherous seas. At a time when many in Europe believed the world was flat, the Spaniards were sailing to the edge of that world. The captains, including Colón, were educated men and believed otherwise, believing they could sail to the Orient. With only their faith and courage, Colón and his men traveled to the known end of the world and beyond. One can only imagine if we would have this same kind of faith and courage.

Although Colón did not find the route to the riches of the Orient, he proved to the Spanish royalty that they could sail the seas. Thus marked the beginning of a new Spanish domination: global sailing and conquest. Spain colonized the Bahaman Islands, then called Hispaniola, for more than twenty years before sending expeditions to the mainland of what is now Mexico. On February 8, 1517, the governor of Cuba, Diego Velásquez, commissioned Francisco Hernández de Córdova to explore the Mexican mainland. The expedition met some resistance by native Indians before it returned to Cuba. However, Governor Velásquez was pleased with the report of the Córdova expedition and commissioned a second expedition led by Juan de Grijalva in the year 1518.

The Grijalva expedition also met resistance from the native Indians, whereby seven Spanish soldiers were killed and sixty were wounded. Grijalva was also wounded and had two of his teeth broken. However, Grijalva returned to Hispaniola and delivered something of the most importance to Governor Velásquez — GOLD. Grijalva also brought information about the mass of land, the Yucatán Peninsula, its cities and this newly discovered country. Grijalva sailed around Yucatán to the shores of the Bay of Campeche discovering the river which now bears his name. Grijalva was the first known navigator to set foot on Mexican soil and credited with the name New Spain. He and his crew mapped the land, rivers, and discovered the island of Cozumel. Grijalva was also the first known European to have contact with the Aztecs.

But rivers and land were secondary to GOLD. Riches and spreading Christianity were the driving forces during this period of exploration. Returning to Spain with gold and other riches brought honor and power to the men who courageously charted this unknown land.

Spanish Conquest of the Aztec Empire

From the reports of the Córdova and Grijalva expeditions, Governor Diego Velásquez believed vast riches lay with the discovery of the new territory. He commissioned another expedition to *conquistador* Hernando Cortés. Cortés, a Spaniard of lesser noble birth, chose to pursue life in the New World. He was in his mid to late thirties and an *alcalde* on the island of Cuba. Velásquez appointed Cortés as Captain General of the third expedition and a larger fleet, much to the dislike of some of the governor's relatives and others who did not believe Cortés was the most qualified. Cortés was renowned for his courage in battle and upon learning his expedition might be stopped used his own personal resources to gather his provisions. He departed Cuba with about eleven ships, five hundred men, sixteen horses, a small number of cannons, and provisions for his horses and men, just as Governor Velásquez was convinced he made a mistake by choosing Cortés and attempted to cancel the expedition.

Author's Note: Some references may use Hernán Cortés, Hernando Cortés, or Ferdinando Cortés when referring to Cortés. This text uses Hernando Cortés.

The Cortés expedition set sail on February 10, 1519, to the island of Cozumel just off the tip of the Yucatán Peninsula. There they found a Spaniard named Jerónimo de Aguilar. Aguilar explained how he and a number of other Spaniards were shipwrecked on their voyage from Spain to Santo Domingo. He and several survivors drifted to Cozumel on a small boat. Aguilar lived on the island of Cozumel as a slave to a *cacique* [ka-sē-k] or Indian chief for the past eight years. In that time he learned the native language and was most helpful to Cortés as an interpreter.

Cortés followed the same route along the eastern coast of Mexico explored and charted by Córdova and Grijalva. Before each battle Cortés would gather his men and they would say Mass. They would commend themselves to their Lord Jesus Christ and the blessed Mother, and with the blessing they felt assured of protection and it put courage into their hearts for the next battle.

As they won battles the soldiers would destroy the Indian's idols and the friars would setup alters, crosses, and convert the tribes to Christianity, teaching them the use of candles and the process of making native wax.

Later when Cortés defeated the Indian warriors at Tabasco, the people gave Cortés twenty Indian women, including a woman named la Malinche. She converted to Christianity and was renamed Doña Marina, or another spelling was Doña Malintzin. She learned Spanish and together Jerónimo de Aguilar and Doña Marina became invaluable as interpreters for Cortés in the conquest of the Aztec empire.

Many of the native tribes encountered by Cortés had been conquered by the strong central Aztec rulers and forced to pay tribute to the Aztec Empire. They rallied with marked resistance against Cortés, but with his superior weapons Cortés prevailed over the Indians. However after each battle was won, Cortés did not excessively kill or enslave the natives. With the help of Aguilar and Doña Marina, Cortés befriended the *caciques* giving them gifts, including beads crafted in Spain. The defeated Indians became Cortés' allies as the Spaniards continued marching inland.

The *caciques* believed the Spaniards, led by Cortés, were Gods. The Indians were taught by their ancestral legends — one day they would be ruled by Gods who came from the direction of the rising sun. The Spaniards had arrived from the east and they came with horses. Not ever having seen a horse before, the Indians thought the Spaniards on horseback were one being, confirming to them the Spaniards were Gods.

Around March 1519, after many battles with Indians and building friendships with the defeated tribes, Cortés founded the first Spanish town in New Spain. He named it Villa Rica de la Vera Cruz, now called Veracruz. So named, because the Cortés expedition arrived at the site on Thursday of the last supper, and landed on Holy Friday of the Cross, and 'rich' because of what was said to Cortés when they landed. "Behold, rich lands!"

From the defeated *caciques* of the Yucatán area, Cortés learned of a rich city called Tenochtitlán [tā-nòch-tēt-län] and about the hated Aztecs ruled buy a great emperor, Prince Montezuma.

Author's Note: Tenochtitlán is now the present day city of Mexico City. Montezuma is the accepted English spelling of the Aztec leader Motecuhzoma or Moctezuma and used in this text.

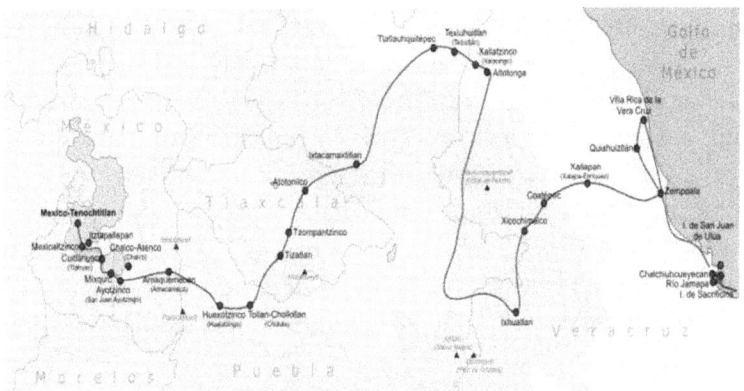

Map of Cortés' route to Tenochtitlán. Image courtesy of Wikipedia Commons under the terms of GNU license.

Through his interpreters, the defeated *caciques* told Cortés they were conquered by the Aztecs and had to pay tribute to the great Montezuma in the form of taxes and slaves. The Aztecs also took their women and slaves for sacrifice. The cunning Cortés promised the *caciques* he would protect them from the Aztecs and proved it by arresting the Aztec tax collectors. The *caciques* gladly accepted this strange man's protection and friendship and it was more through alliances, not war, that Cortés continued exploring this foreign land.

After interrogating the tax collectors about the great city of Tenochtitlán and Prince Montezuma, Cortés released them sending them home. Montezuma sent several ambassadors to meet with Cortés. They brought him beautiful gifts of golden idols in the shape of animals, green feathers, and rich cotton cloth rolls. Montezuma sent these ambassadors to understand the strange men and was probably both curious and fearful.

Cortés told them to tell their Prince Montezuma they were Christians and they came from a distant land by order of their Lord King Carlos (1516 – 1556), the greatest Lord on earth. Cortés acknowledged the great prince who ruled over their land and told the ambassadors to tell their leader he wished to be friends with the great Prince Montezuma. Giving the ambassadors glass beads from Spain on behalf of King Carlos, he explained through his interpreters the Spaniards wished to trade and make friends with the Aztecs.

Cortés asked the ambassadors where and when their prince would meet with him. The ambassadors replied:

> "You have only just now arrived and you already ask to speak with our prince; accept now this present which

we give you in his name and afterwards you will tell me what you think fitting."[3]

Cortés accepted their response and the ambassadors returned to Tenochtitlán to report to their prince, Montezuma.

After hearing the report from his ambassadors, Montezuma had his priests sacrifice several Indian slaves to Huitzilopochtli [wētz-ē-loh-posh-t-lē], the God of War and Sacrifice, and to Mictlantecuhtli [mēkt-lahn-teh-koot-lē], the God of Hell. Through the interpretation of his priests, this Aztec ritual provided Montezuma an answer from the Gods — keep the strangers out of Tenochtitlán and make war on them.

Nevertheless, Montezuma was hesitant about making war on Cortés. He also believed the Spaniards were Gods who came from the rising sun to rule the land and people, as prophesy had foretold. Instead of war, Montezuma kept sending ambassadors with gifts asking Cortés to accept the gifts for his Lord King Carlos and suggesting he should leave the country. Cortés and his men were not leaving, but continuing their exploration.

The Aztecs controlled vast portions of land and had many tribes under their domination. It is believed the Aztec Empire controlled 11 million people over a wide spread area of what is now Mexico. The Aztecs warriors had won these lands through force and Montezuma was not afraid of war. While he sent ambassadors to make peace, he also sent tribes from his kingdom to attack the Spaniards.

At times, Cortés and his soldiers were outnumbered by thousands of Indian warriors and it seemed they would be easily defeated, but the Spaniards were not weak or frightened of war. These were men of great courage, men who had traveled across the Atlantic Ocean. With this great courage they would dig deep into their souls and pray to their Lord and Saviour Jesus Christ to send Santiago, the War Saint, to help them defeat the Indians. The Spaniards with their superior weapons and great valor won many battles, but not without losing some of their soldiers and horses and having many wounded. Captured Spaniards were killed and sacrificed to the Aztec Gods, their arms and legs eaten by the Aztec warriors to devour their strength.

Montezuma continued sending ambassadors with gifts to Cortés, hoping to dissuade the Spaniards from entering Tenochtitlán. Likewise, he kept sending warriors to make war on the intruders. This game went on until Cortés and his soldiers finally marched into Tenochtitlán.

On November 8, 1519, the Spaniards glimpsed their first sight of the grand city of Tenochtitlán. Cortés and his soldiers saw wonders they had never seen before. Tenochtitlán was truly an impressive city rising from the land, surrounded by a lake. On the causeways there were many bridges and the lake was crowded with canoes. At this time the Spaniards numbered about four hundred soldiers. Cortés remembered the warnings given him by the Huexotzingo [wah-shot-sen-go] and Tlaxcala [t-lak-se-kala] *caciques* — beware of entering Tenochtitlán. The *caciques* warned they would be captured, sacrificed, and eaten once the Aztecs had them inside the city.

The bravery of the Spaniards as they forged ahead into the unknown and dangerous Tenochtitlán is remarkable. What nature of men have there been in the world who have shown such daring?

Cortés described his first meeting with Montezuma [Moctezuma] in a letter to King Carlos of Spain:

There came to meet me at this place [on a causeway] nearly a thousand of

the principal inhabitants of the great city, all uniformly dressed according to their custom in very rich costumes; and as soon as they had come within speaking distance, each one, as he approached me, performed a salutation in much use among them, by placing his hand upon the ground and kissing it; and thus I was kept waiting about an hour, until all had performed the ceremony. Connected with the city is a wooden bridge ten paces wide, where the causeway is open to allow the water free ingress and egress, as it rises and falls; and also for the security of the city, as they can remove the long and wide beams of which the bridge is formed, and replace them whenever they wish; and there are many such bridges in different parts of the city, as your Highness will perceive hereafter from the particular account I shall give of it.

  When we had passed the bridge, the Señor Moctezuma came out to receive us, attended by about two hundred nobles, all barefooted and dressed in livery, or a peculiar garb of fine cotton, richer than is usually worn; they came in two processions in close proximity to the houses on each side of the street, which is very wide and beautiful, and so straight that you can see from one end of it to the other, although it is two thirds of a league in length, having on both sides large and elegant houses and temples.

  Moctezuma came through the center of the street, attended by two lords, one upon his right, and the other upon his left hand, one of whom was the same nobleman who, as I have mentioned, came to meet me in a litter; and the other was the brother of Moctezuma, lord of the city of Iztapalapa, which I had left the same day; all three were dressed in the same manner, except that Moctezuma wore shoes, while the others were without them. He was supported on the arms of both, and as we approached, I alighted and advanced alone to salute him; but the two attendant lords stopped me to prevent my touching him, and they and he both performed the ceremony of kissing the ground; after which he directed his brother who accompanied him to remain with me; the, latter accordingly took me by the arm, while Moctezuma, with his other attendant, walked a short distance in front of me, and after he had spoken to me, all the other nobles also came up to address me, and then went away in two processions with great regularity, one after the other, and in this manner returned to the city.

At the time I advanced to speak to Moctezuma, I took off from myself a collar of pearls and glass diamonds, and put it around his neck. After having proceeded along the street, one of his servants came bringing two collars formed of shell fish, enclosed in a roll of cloth, which were made from the shells of colored prawns or periwinkles, held by them in high estimation; and from each collar depended eight golden prawns, finished in a very perfect manner, about a foot and a half in length. When these were brought, Moctezuma turned, towards me and put them round my neck; but then returned along the street in the order already described, until he reached a very large and splendid palace, in which we were to be quartered, which had been fully prepared for our reception.[4]

This brief synopsis of history illustrates the courage and tenacity of the Spaniards, specifically one man, Hernando Cortés. Knowing he was greatly outnumbered, Cortés orchestrated a daring event. During his stay in the city of Tenochtitlán, Cortés invited the prince to visit with him. He took the Aztec Prince Montezuma prisoner and placed him under Spanish guard within his own city. With Montezuma under his control, Cortés protected himself and his soldiers from the Aztec army and people.

While in Tenochtitlán, Cortés received a message from Vera Cruz. The governor of Cuba, Diego Velásquez, was sending a large force to arrest him. Cortés had made this entire exploration and conquest without authorization from the Spanish governor. Little did the governor know Cortés and his men discovered vast treasures held by Montezuma. Shortly after their arrival in Tenochtitlán, they held Montezuma captive and controlled his treasures.

Cortés took half of his soldiers and headed to Vera Cruz leaving his trusted captain Pedro de Alvarado in Tenochtitlán. Alvarado and his men were ordered to guard Montezuma and the riches and treasures they gathered from their victories and looted from Montezuma.

In Vera Cruz, Cortés defeated the Spaniards sent by Governor Velásquez in battle. Again the cunning Cortés used the defeat to his advantage. He enticed Velásquez's men into joining him and won them over to his side by promising them riches beyond their dreams. When he marched back to Tenochtitlán, Cortés had a larger army, an army hungry for riches and gold.

On his return to Tenochtitlán he found his Captain Pedro de Alvarado and his troops barricaded in their quarters and surrounded by the Aztec army. Captain Alvarado explained to Cortés he discovered a plot by the Aztecs to capture the intruders and sacrifice them to their Gods. Alvarado attacked the Aztecs while they were celebrating in front of their idols, a ritual Alvarado believed was to precede the Aztec's attack on the Spaniards. Alvarado's brutal attack killed many innocent Aztec people, including women and children.

The people of Tenochtitlán were outraged and blamed Montezuma, their protector and leader. Losing all respect for the great Montezuma his people stoned him to death. Surprisingly, without the great Montezuma, the Aztec people did what their exulted ruler had not. They attacked Cortés and his men. The Spaniards fought their way out of Tenochtitlán, losing many soldiers and many others were seriously wounded. They lost most of their plundered treasure, but managed to escape.

Cortés regrouped and on May 21, 1521, and with the help from his Indian allies began the siege on Tenochtitlán. Cuauhtémoc [cuau-ha-tém-oc], the new Lord of Tenochtitlán, vowed to the people he would defeat the enemy or they would all die fighting. The siege lasted eighty-five days. Cuauhtémoc was true to his words and they fought the Spanish troops with tremendous courage. The Spaniards fought against incredible odds. With their superior weapons they prevailed over the Aztecs, took Tenochtitlán, and captured Cuauhtémoc. The Aztec empire was defeated. This tremendous feat by Cortés and his Spanish soldiers changed the history of the Americas and created a new territory for the Spanish Empire, commonly called New Spain. For his efforts, Cortés was appointed Marqués del Valle de Oaxaca by the Spanish crown.

One has to admire the Spanish *conquistadores* for their unwavering faith and courage. In a land far and foreign from their home, they explored and fought against overwhelming odds of nature and man. They survived with an unwavering faith in their Saviour Jesus Christ and their absolute loyalty to the Spanish Crown. In a world dominated by brute power and resources, the Spanish descended upon the New World to extract natural resources and to spread Catholicism, which helped Spain become the most powerful empire in Europe by 1600.

It was with these brave *conquistadores* that Elfego's earliest known ancestors came to the Americas. Several de Vacas came to the New World shortly after the discovery and creation of New Spain. The original spelling of Elfego's family name was 'Vaca,' but by the seventeenth century 'Baca' had become the common spelling. It was derived from 'Cabeza de Vaca,' a title and name received by a Spanish hero in the year 1212.

Documented during Cortés' time were Diego de Vaca, a native of Mancilla in León, and Luis Vaca, a native of Toledo. Either of these could have been the father or grandfather of Juan de Vaca, believed to be Elfego's earliest known ancestor in New Spain. The Vacas who came from Spain to colonize New Spain were Spaniards who came to the New World and prospered, living at first in Mexico City and later moving north into the New Mexico Territory. They stayed in New Spain to become a prominent family bloodline and eventually becoming Americans. Little is known about why they might have come to New Spain — adventure? riches? land? No one knows, however, in a wild and harsh world the Vacas came and they survived.

More than three hundred and sixty years after his ancestors took their first steps in the New World, Elfego Baca would find himself in Upper Frisco Plaza defending Hispanic villagers from foul play and harassment. Sheltered only by a mud shack he fought for thirty-six hours with only his wits, two colt six-shooters, and a statue of *Nuestra Señora Santa Ana,* Our Lady of Saint Anne, for protection. Like his *conquistador* ancestors, he prevailed and he survived!

Life in New Spain

New Spain was ruled by a viceroyalty, a Spanish colonial administrative district under the control of Spain, given the responsibility of ruling territories of the Spanish Empire in the Americas from 1535 to 1821. Antonio de Mendoza was the first of sixty viceroys who ruled New Spain for three centuries. By the early 1800s, New Spain encompassed the vast area we now know as the southwestern United States, stretching from the Mississippi River to the Canadian border. It also claimed central and southern Mexico extending to southern parts of the South American continent.

Map of New Spain circa 1819. Image courtesy of Wikipedia Commons under the terms of GNU license.

Even in the early years of Spanish rule, New Spain was an enormous territory, diverse in both terrain and native peoples. Travel and communication was difficult and yet the Spaniards continued their spread into the wildernesses of what is now the United States southwest and Central America.

In letters translated by the National Humanities Center, settlers seemed to write of loneliness, but mostly of prosperity:

> Antonio Mateos writes to his wife in Spain in 1558, "The land is the most luxuriant, and plenteous and abundant in grain. . . . Food provisions are cheap here, and things from Spain are expensive."

> Andrés García writes to his nephew in New Castile, Spain in 1571, "Nephew, I live in Mexico City in the tiánguiz of San Juan, among the shops of Tegada. I deal in Campeche wood and cotton blankets and wax, and I also have a certain business in cacao [cocoa] in Soconusco."

> Maria de Caranza writes to her brother in Spain in 1589, "It would be a greater happiness to see you, yet you want to stay there in that poverty and need which people suffer in Spain."

> Fray Juan de Mora, Augustinian priest in Mexico City, writes to his brothers in Spain 1574, "Let him who should want to come understand that he must be a man who can assert himself on his own, by his own good industry and diligence, as many others do here and make their fortunes."

The letters imply food was abundant and cheap, while goods from Spain were expensive. The letter from Maria de Caranza refers to the poverty and suffering in Spain and implies life in the New World may be better and fortunes could be made, especially by pure-blooded Spaniards.

To understand New Spain, one must understand the social and legal *casta* system of the new territory. Spanish royalty only trusted Spaniards of pure blood, meaning a Spaniard born in Spain. Spaniards born in Spain were known as *Peninsulares,* who were the highest social status in New Spain. Only *Peninsulares* were given viceroyalties and other high-level government positions. Next were Spaniards of pure blood lines, but born in New Spain. Spaniards born in New Spain were referred to as *Criollos.* Although of pure Spanish blood lines, the *Criollo* class, ranked below the Iberian *Peninsulares* simply because they were not born in Spain. The caste system was so important to the power structure of New Spain that women colonists often endured the harsh trip across the Atlantic to give birth to their children in Spain.

Indians or the natives of New Spain ranked below the *Criollo* class. For obvious reasons a new racial category emerged as a mixed-race people. The term *mestizo* became a racial category in New Spain's caste system. A *mestizo* was any person born of mixed blood, a Spanish parent and an Indian parent, and then continued offspring. *Mestizos* were considered the lowest of the social classes.

When a baby was baptized they were assigned for life to a caste by the baptismal priest, therefore making the baptismal priest very important. He decided and declared at the baptism to which caste the baby belonged for life. This led to corruption in the priesthood. Social status could be bribed or lost, depending upon the local priest.

So important was the social caste system in New Spain, families carefully maintained their family records for the purpose of ensuring documented blood lines. The Catholic Church also provided detailed records of births, deaths, baptisms, etc. Because of this detailed record keeping, genealogical information is available today and gives us great insight into the growth and movement of the colonists for hundreds of years. Without the social caste system's importance and the Catholic Church these records would be long lost.

Gachupín was a name the Aztecs gave the Spanish *conquistadores*. Since they had never seen a horse or a man on horseback wearing spurs, the only Indian word in their language was *gachupín,* meaning 'the man wearing shoes with pins.' This referred to the spurs they wore when riding their horses. The name *Gachupín* became commonly used to refer to the *Peninsulares* class or Spaniards born in Spain.

Gachupínes ruled New Spain with an iron fist. As the governing land and business owners, they enslaved the Indians and *mestizos* to work their haciendas and mines. *Criollos* had many of the same privileges as *Gachupínes* in regard to land ownership, however they were not allowed to govern New Spain in high-ranking positions. Indians, blacks, and *mestizos,* or mixed bloods, had few rights and were either slaves or indentured workers. *Mestizos* were generally the lowest social status, while over generations becoming the largest class of people. Although evolving over time, this governmental and social caste system lasted almost three hundred years, but as history has taught us many times — the natives got restless.

Searching for the Seven Cities of Gold

New Mexico's history is unique as well as fascinating. In 1540, some eighty years before the Pilgrims landed at Plymouth Rock in 1620 on the east coast of what is now Massachusetts, Coronado came to New Mexico looking for gold, the fabled 'seven cities of gold.' However, the history of New Mexico started many years before Coronado came looking for gold:

> In prehistoric days, much of New Mexico sat underneath a vast sea that covered a great portion of the Southwest, and giant dinosaurs roamed freely across whatever existing tropical landscape rested above water. Ultimately, the giant reptiles vanished, the sea receded, and glaciers from the last ice age melted, carving out the high mountains found in many regions of the state today. The Clovis-Paleo Indians later discovered the eastern plains of New Mexico, the same expansive romping grounds of the dinosaurs around 10,000 BC.[5]

A devastating flood hit Folsom in northeastern New Mexico in 1908. When the site was later excavated by archaeologists in the early 1920s, a spear point was found embedded in a mastodon bone. Modern-age civilizations, or the 'ancients' as they are more appropriately called, have been discovered throughout New Mexico dating to 1000 BC.

The Anasazi tribes or ancient puebloans built and lived at Chaco Canyon and other sites starting around 1050 AD. The land was lush and more hospitable than the plains, with good water sources, lush grasslands, and forests. The high mesas gave the ancients protection from raiding tribes.

After several centuries of migration throughout the canyon lands, the Acoma Indian tribe settled in the 1100s on a mesa about sixty miles west of Albuquerque. This early founding date makes the Acoma Pueblo, now commonly known as Sky City, one of the earliest continuously inhabited communities in the United States. Sky City continues to thrive as the heart and soul of the Acoma tribe today. Structures dating to the 1600s are still in use today as living history and tours are made available to tourists. The spires of the San Esteban del Ray Mission is one of the top 100 National Historic Treasures.

San Esteban del Rey Mission as it looks today at Sky City, NM. Photograph taken by the author, 2016.

Destined to Survive

The puebloan peoples were not roaming tribes moving with the weather and food as might have been found in the plains states of Texas and the midwest. These ancient people developed sophisticated cities and organized social structures, which are still very visible today at such archaeological sites as Chaco Canyon.

To irrigate their crops, the Chacoans developed sophisticated techniques for capturing rainwater. They created a system of dams, canals, and ditches to collect runoff from the sloping cliffs above the canyon, and redirected the water onto leveled gardens on the canyon floor. Unknown to these peaceful puebloans, the Spaniards were landing in the Bahamas and the march to the north would begin.

While the Spaniards worked to rebuild Tenochtitlán into present day Mexico City, other explorers continued discovering new territory to the north and northwest of the Mexico mainland. In April of 1528 Pánfilo de Narváez arrived on the west coast of Florida, near what now is St. Petersburg. Narváez met with disaster fighting natives while trekking north to the panhandle of Florida. With no ships, Narváez ordered his men to build rafts for their return to New Spain. On their return trip a storm destroyed the rafts. Only eighty-six men survived and were able to swim ashore.

Those eighty-six men started an overland trek to New Spain. Most of them died of starvation and some died from attacks by natives and illness. Only four men survived: Álvar Núñez Cabeza de Vaca, Alonso del Castillo Maldonado, Andrés Dorantes de Carranza and his Berber slave Estevanico. Their adventure over land took eight years to reach the outposts of New Spain. Their trek followed the Gulf of Mexico and along the Rio Grande into California and then south until they reached Mexico

City. The men brought tales they heard from the natives of great cities of gold to the north.

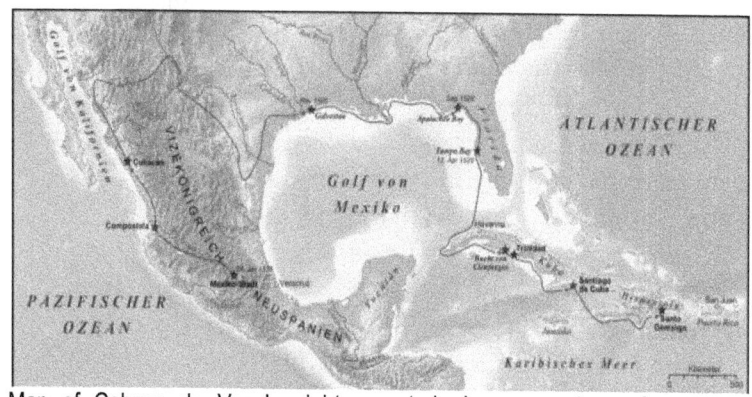

Map of Cabeza de Vaca's eight year trek. Image courtesy of Wikipedia Commons under the terms of GNU license.

Imagine Cabeza de Vaca exploring the American southeast and across the southern plains for eight years. It certainly should make us realize these men were tough Spanish *hombres*!

The journey of Cabeza de Vaca remains one of the most amazing feats of courage, grit, and determination of the exploration of the Americas, although relatively little celebrated in American history. His accounts of the journey are the earliest written descriptions of the American Southwest. As compared to Coronado, Cortés, Columbus, and de Soto, Cabeza de Vaca is not as well known or documented in American history books.

The correct spelling of Elfego Baca's family name is Vaca. Álvar Cabeza de Vaca was born before 1490 in Jerez de la Frontera, Spain, into a *hidalgo* family of Spanish nobility. It is possible Cabeza de Vaca was an ancestor or relative of Elfego Baca. Elfego's known direct lineage, through Juan de Vaca's ancestors, is believed to have come to New Spain in the early 1500s. Regardless of whether Álvar is a direct ancestor of Elfego, they seem to possess similar courageous traits with both men surviving unbelievable odds.

Sometime in 1536, Cabeza de Vaca and his three companions reached the northern settlement of Culiacán ending their eight year, thousand mile trek up Florida through Texas and New Mexico, with stories of rich Indian settlements. Intrigued, Viceroy Mendoza sent Fray Marcos de Niza north to verify Cabeza de Vaca's story. The fray returned and reported he saw from a distance the first of the Seven Cities of Gold, called Cibola. Viceroy Mendoza relied on his trusted friend Francisco Vasquez de Coronado to form an expedition and go north to conquer the new land identified by Cabeza de Vaca.

The reports of great golden cities raised Coronado's interest. At the time, Coronado was governor of Nueva Galicia, which is now Sinaloa, Mexico. In 1540 he organized a large prestigious expedition of 300 Spaniards, 300 Indians, and 1000 slaves. On February 22, 1540, exactly 192 years before George Washington was born, Coronado and his entourage departed Compostela, Nueva Galicia, with great fanfare and a gala ceremony in the Spanish tradition for such important events. Following the writings and accounts of Cabeza de Vaca's incredible adventure, Coronado, with Fray Marcos de Niza as a guide, headed north.

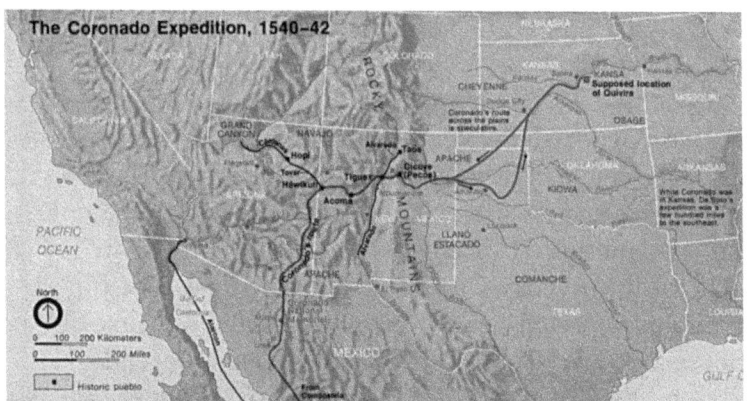
Map of Coronado's route into New Mexico. Image courtesy of Wikipedia Commons under the terms of GNU license.

One member of Coronado's expedition was Elfego Baca's ancestor, Juan de Vaca, a colonist born in Mexico City, a *Criollo*. It is not known in what capacity he joined the expedition, although one might expect he was a military man, since Coronado's intent was to conquer and plunder the Seven Cities of Gold. Juan de Vaca survived the two year adventure returning to Mexico City.

Coronado met with disappointment when his expedition reached Cibola in the west of what is now New Mexico. Cibola was simply a Zuni Indian pueblo and not a great golden city reported by Fray Marcos de Niza. Continuing north, Coronado traveled as far as present-day Kansas looking for the seven cities of Cibola.

Although Coronado did not find gold, he explored much of the Southwest, finding it hospitable and charting it for future exploration. Upon returning to Nueva Galicia in 1542, unhealthy and without treasure from his trip north, he reassumed the governorship until 1544.

In 1595, twenty-five years before the Pilgrims landed on North America and began an English colony, Don Juan de Oñate was awarded a contract by King Phillip II of Spain and governorship for the settlement of New Mexico.

Oñate was a wealthy Spaniard who was battle tested and also educated in mining. The Spanish treasury was primarily interested in gold and silver mines in New Spain and Oñate's mining experience made him a logical choice:

> Juan de Oñate grew up in both Pánuco, a mining town near Zacatecas, and Mexico City, therefore learning the mining industry and the social graces and refinements of being a caballero. His father, Cristóbal de Oñate was recognized by Viceroy Mendoza and the Spanish Royalty for dependable leadership. These qualities and family responsibilities would one day be passed on to his son Juan.[6]

As an aside, Juan de Oñate married Isabel de Tolosa Cortés Montezuma, the granddaughter of conquistador Hernando Cortés and his Aztec mistress Isabel Montezuma. Isabel Montezuma was the offspring of the Aztec emperor Montezuma and one of his mistresses. Their first child was born in the 1590s in Mexico City and was named Cristóbal after Juan's father.

For leading the expedition Oñate was granted titles and honors:

> . . . Oñate was granted the titles of governor and captain general for two generations on condition that he fulfill his part of the contract. The viceroy promised to supplicate the king to extend this period an equal length of time. He was also to have the title of

adelantado on taking possession of the land. This honor was to endure as long as the governorship, and Velasco agreed to seek a similar extension of the office.

Under the terms of the contract, Oñate was obliged to recruit at his own cost a minimum of 200 men, who were fully equipped with supplies and provisions. He also provided 1000 head of cattle, 3000 sheep for wool and another 100 sheep for mutton, 1000 goats, 150 colts, 150 mares, and ample quantities of flour, corn, jerked beef, and sowing wheat. Supplies for the settlement, horse shoes, footwear, gifts to the Indians, cloth, paper, iron tools and many other supplies were readied at Oñate's expense.[7]

Oñate expended a tremendous personal cost to undertake this expedition. He was promised honor, status, and political office, something reserved in New Spain to nobility or *hidalgos*. To assume this level of status, Oñate made sure to travel in style:

Due to Spanish politics in Mexico Oñate's expedition was delayed several times. It wasn't until January 26, 1598 when Oñate and the colonists headed north having all the documents approved and satisfied by the royal government. Juan de Oñate's dream of conquering new lands and becoming the first governor of New Mexico soon came true. The regal expedition was carefully organized for Oñate's comfort. As part of his personal equipment he took 25 horses and 25 mules fitted with harnesses. Two luxury coaches, two iron carts, leather saddles and shields, lances, halberds, coats of mail and helmets with beavers, horse armor, harquebuses and many swords, daggers and other fighting weapons.[8]

One can only imagine the trials and hardships Oñate's long caravan traveling through deserts, mountains, and crossing rivers for over five hundred miles encountered. It was estimated the caravan started with about five hundred people. The true spirit of the adventurous Spaniard was in display here. In reality, they were headed into an unknown and dangerous country, but Oñate would prove to be a staunch and aggressive leader:

> . . . when Oñate's army reached the Conchos it encamped on the shore. One hundred and twenty-nine soldiers, eighty-three wagons, and seven thousand head of stock had to cross the river. No one dared tempt the rushing stream. Seeing the fainthearted soldiers lag Oñate mounted a charger and made a stirring challenge to his men. Then he spurred his horse into the river and soon gained the opposite bank. Returning to the army he took the lead in goading the stock across the stream. One incident in this scene called forth a novel plan.

> When the sheep were driven into the water, many sank as the wool became water soaked. To remedy this tragic situation the governor ordered his astonished followers to construct a bridge. It was a primitive pontoon structure. Two dozen cart wheels were placed in the stream some distance apart and secured by ropes. Trees were felled, stripped of branches, and placed on top of the wheels. A layer of brush and sticks was added, then a covering of earth, and the bridge was completed. The sheep crossed dry-shod, and the structure was quickly destroyed as night settled on the scene.[9]

The first pueblos encountered by Oñate were the Piro pueblo Indians located in central New Mexico along the Rio Grande. The Piros left the pueblo and went into hiding when they saw Oñate and his fantastic caravan approaching. Oñate sent the Piros gifts of simple trinkets. From one of the largest Piro pueblos, the *cacique* finally greeted Oñate. He gave Oñate large amounts of corn to prove his friendship. Oñate named the location Socorro, meaning 'giving help or aid.' Both the Piro Indians and the site Oñate named Socorro survive today. Socorro, New Mexico, became the county seat of Socorro County and the city where Elfego Baca would be born more than two and a half centuries later.

Memorial sculpture in Socorro Heritage Plaza, Socorro, New Mexico commemorating the town's establishment in 1598. Photograph taken by the author, 2012.

On July 11, 1598, Juan de Oñate established the first capital of New Mexico and named it San Juan de los Caballeros. The site was approximately twenty-five miles north of present-day Santa Fe, on the Rio Grande just north of the confluence with the Chama River and near one of the largest settlements of the Tewa Pueblos. The surrounding land was rich for growing crops and the vistas of the Sangre de Cristo mountain range pleased him. To anchor the new town, the first church was quickly built:

> . . . San Juan Baptista [sic] was begun on August 23 and completed in fifteen days so the dedicatory exercises could be observed September 8. The occasion was a festive one, and in their amusement the Spanish gallants demonstrated how much of the crusading spirit still coursed in their veins. To honor the event what else was appropriate but a sham battle, the soldiers being divided into opposing groups labeled Moors and Christians. The latter fought on horseback with lances and shields, while the former were on foot and used muskets.[10]

The festivities at San Juan Bautista included a ritual dance still conducted today for special occasions. Some believe the dance portrays the triumph of good over evil, or the holy virgin's conversion of the pagan king. Others allude to a hidden transcript of native regeneration and resistance against foreign invaders. Some scholars trace the dance to the *morisca*, a dance said to have originated in Medieval Spain in the twelfth century or earlier as a pantomime of Moorish-Christian combat. Encounter, struggle, and transformation between light and dark forces is a story for all times and places, whether Medieval Spain, sixteenth century Mexico, or New Mexico today.

Once the capital was settled, Governor Oñate turned his efforts to exploring his kingdom and the priests went about converting Indians to Christianity. Oñate would gather his top captains and elite soldiers along with priests and visit every pueblo within his realm.

On one trip he found the mesa-top pueblo, the home of the Acoma Indians. The mesa was four hundred feet tall and not easily accessible. One of the minor chiefs, Zutucapán, gathered a war party to kill the intruders, however he was out voted by the other chiefs who gave the Spaniards food and water. Sometime later Zutucapán became the head *cacique* over the Acoma people and vowed to drive the Spaniards out of New Mexico. Zutucapán ordered a surprise attack on a visiting troop of Spaniards. People threw stones and war clubs down at the soldiers. Zutucapán himself killed Juan de Zaldívar, one of Oñate's relatives and a trusted soldier.

News of the Acoma rebellion reached San Juan. This first Indian uprising frightened the colonists. On January 10, 1599, Governor Oñate assembled his army to assess the Acoma situation. The soldiers worried about the safety of their families and told Governor Oñate, unless the rebellion was crushed, they would return to New Spain. The Governor listened to them and wasted no time in organizing an army to deal with the Acomas:

> And so, by with the agreement of his priests, Oñate reached a decision and war was ordained, sealing the fate of the Acoma. With a clear conscience Juan de Oñate declared "war by blood and fire" (guerra de sangre y fuego) against the hapless Acoma Indians. That was a phrase habitually used in the Moorish crusades and employed just as regularly

by the Oñates and other frontier captains in their drawn-out conflicts with the Chichimecas. It meant all Indians were enemies of the Spanish Crown and would be punished, pursued, subjugated, enslaved or exterminated.[11]

Governor Oñate asked *Sargento Mayor* Vincente de Zaldívar to lead the battle. Vincente was the brother of Juan de Zaldívar, who had been killed by the Acomas. Like their *conquistador* ancestors, faith prevailed for the Spaniards. One of Zaldívar's soldiers would corroborate a story told by the Indians. They saw a Spaniard on a white horse gallop out of the smoke yielding a flaming sword and a beautiful maiden rode at his side. Zaldívar and his men believed Santiago, the Spanish War God, and the Virgin Mary had intervened on their behalf to guarantee their success.

Zaldívar brought many prisoners to San Juan, where Governor Oñate immediately put them on trial. He appointed a defense attorney for the accused along with interpreters to assist the Indians. Oñate held the trial at the Santo Domingo pueblo, mainly to impress the Indians not to rebel and suffer the consequences:

About 500 prisoners were taken and later sentenced to a variety of punishments. Don Oñate ordered that every male above the age of twenty-five would have their right foot cut off and be enslaved for a period of twenty years. However, only twenty-four men actually received amputations. Males between the age of twelve and twenty-five were also enslaved for twenty years along with all of the females above the age of twelve. Many of these natives were dispersed among the residences of government officials or at Franciscan missions. Sixty of the youngest women were deemed not guilty and sent to Mexico City where they were sent to Catholic convents.[12]

The form of punishment administered by the Spaniards shocked the pueblos and fostered great resentment amongst the Indians. Governor Oñate got his message across however — rebellion against the Spaniards would be met with swift retaliation. The relationship between the Spaniards and the Indians would be forever changed. The Acomas felt the wrath of their new masters, but within a year or two most of them escaped their servitude and returned to the mesa and rebuilt their pueblo, which still stands to this day.

At the end of the 1500s, sometime between 1598 to 1600, Oñate relocated his headquarters and colonists across the Rio Grande to the village of Yunque, which he renamed the village of San Gabriel. Desperate to save the struggling colony, Oñate sent messages and other documents to the viceroy in Mexico City in March 1599. The messages asked for fortifications to the settlement in the form of settlers, soldiers and friars, and badly-needed supplies to nourish his hungry colony. Answering the call to join the settlers was Elfego Baca's ancestor:

> The direct Elfego Baca family line in New Mexico dates back to Capitán Cristóbal Baca, who came to reinforce Don Juan de Oñate's New Mexican colony in 1600. He was the son of Juan

de Vaca, born in Mexico City, who explored New Mexico with Coronado's expedition in 1540.

Capitán Cristóbal Baca and his wife Doña Ana Ortiz brought three grown daughters and one young boy to the new colony of New Mexico. The son was named Antonio, and daughters were Juana, Isabel, and María. A second son, Alonso, was the first Baca born in New Mexico.[13]

Colonists were motivated by the eternal Spanish quest for fame and riches. Governor Oñate was parceling out grants of *encomienda*, blocks of pueblos that would have to pay yearly tribute to the Spaniards. Oñate's settlers who remained in New Mexico would gain the coveted glory of becoming *hidalgo*. Attaining *hidalgo* status was an honor, a designation of *caballero* or knight with the right to use the title of *Don [de origen noble]*, in front of one's family name, and so it would be for Captain Cristóbal Baca who would attain the title of *Don*.

Governor Oñate would send small troops of soldiers out to prospect for silver and gold, finding little to support the colony. The early New Mexican colonists, including the Bacas, only managed to scratch out a meager living at this northern-most outpost. San Gabriel served as the capital of New Mexico until the village of Santa Fe was established and the seat of government moved there in 1610, long after Oñate had left the territory.

Communication was difficult in the 1600s. On an ancient east-west trail in western New Mexico a large sandstone rock formation, El Morro, rose from the high desert and could be seen for some distance. The location provided shelter and water, originally named Agua de la

Peña. It also provided a communication board for travelers, who recorded their travels and relayed messages by carving into the soft sandstone rock.

Explorers and travelers have known of the pool by the great rock for centuries. A valuable water source and resting place, many who passed by inscribed their names and messages in the rock next to petroglyphs left by ancient Puebloans. The ruins of a large pueblo located on top of El Morro were vacated by the time the Spaniards arrived in the late 1500s, and its inhabitants may have moved to the nearby pueblos in Zuni and Acoma. As the American west grew in population, El Morro became a break along the trail for those passing through and today is a destination for sightseers. As the popularity of the area increased, so did the tradition of carving inscriptions on the rock. To preserve the historical importance of the area and initiate preservation efforts on the old inscriptions, El Morro was established as a national monument by a presidential proclamation on December 8, 1906.

Don Juan de Oñate's inscription at El Morro in 1605 is the oldest dated inscription, made on his return trip from the Gulf of California:

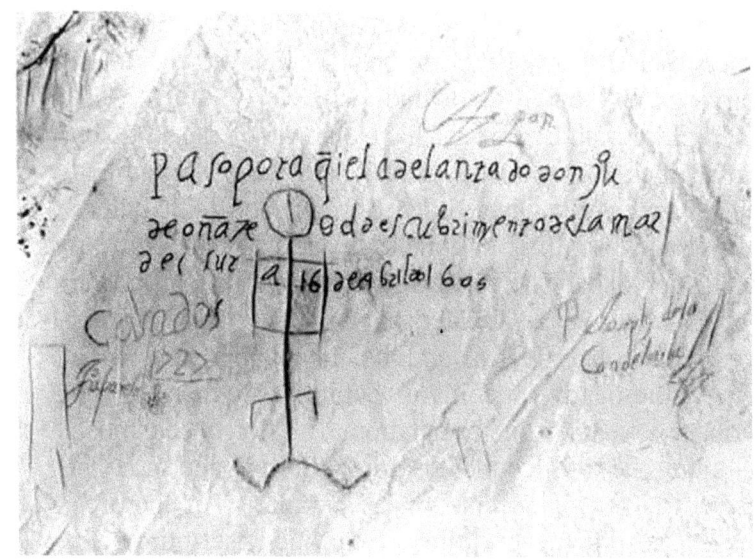

Juan de Oñate inscription, dated 1605 "paso por aq[u]i el adelantado don ju[an] oñate del descubrimiento de la mar del sur a 16 de Abril de 1605". English translation: Governor Don Juan de Oñate passed through here, from the discovery of the Sea of the South on the 16th of April, 1605.[14]

Despite turbulence in the government, the king continued to support the colonization of the new province and Governor Peralta established Santa Fe as the new capital and in 1610 began construction of the Palace of the Governors. The Palace of Governors continues to grace one side of the Santa Fe Plaza National Historic Landmark, Santa Fe, New Mexico.

Life was hard in Santa Fe and the colonists endured many hardships, but they remained in this small Spanish outpost. It is not known if Captain Cristóbal Baca was already entitled to the status of *Don*, as he was always referred to by his military rank of Captain. If not, he should have earned the title of *Don*, as was the agreement with Oñate and his colonists. Captain [*Don*] Cristóbal Baca lived in Santa Fe until his death in 1613.

Though life was hard for the colonists, it was probably harder for the native Indians. By 1680, the pueblos had been under Spanish rule for more than eighty years, frustrated with Spanish protection and the intrusion of the Catholic Church. The church forbade local dances of *kachinas* and intimidated or killed tribal medicine men. Franciscan priest Fray Juan Pío left from Santa Fe on the morning of August 10, 1680, to say Mass at the pueblo of Tesuque. He was there to celebrate the Feast Day of San Lorenzo. When he arrived, he discovered a Spanish settler living in Tesuque had been murdered. Before the fray could report back to Santa Fe, he and about four hundred Spaniards, including twenty Franciscan priests were killed by the Indians.

The Pueblo Indians of the area united and revolted against their colonizers led by a medicine man by the name of Popé. They looted homes, destroyed churches, and burned any signs of the Spanish culture, including government documents. The Pueblo Revolt, sometimes called the Popé Rebellion, had begun. The approximately twelve hundred surviving Spaniards, including the Baca family, fled south to El Paso where they found safe haven. The Indians were victorious and New Mexico was without Spanish rule for the next twelve years.

Around the early 1690s Spain was concerned with losing New Mexico to other European countries, especially France. Diego José de Vargas Zapata Luján Ponce de León y Contreras was chosen by the crown to reconquer New Mexico. In August of 1692, after spending eighteen months in El Paso, Don Diego de Vargas led a force of two hundred soldiers and Indians north to Santa Fe.

On Vargas' return he found many pueblo Indians occupying Santa Fe and began negotiations. When they refused his efforts of negotiation, he threatened to cut off their water supply. The Indians had only one demand.

They named specific Spaniards who should not be allowed to return to New Mexico. Vargas accepted the demand, and then told them to submit and be pardoned or suffer an attack from his formidable army.

Peace between the Indians and Spaniards continued to be tested. Don Diego de Vargas prevailed after each skirmish until Santa Fe was reconquered. At one point he ordered about seventy Indians to be executed and women and children put to servitude. Similar bloody fighting occurred at many of the other pueblos before de Vargas felt the native people had truly submitted to Spanish control and the King's authority. The end of widespread hostilities did not mean an end to Pueblo resentment over continued heavy-handed treatment by the colonists. The plundering of Pueblo stocks of corn and other supplies to sustain the struggling colony was a periodic occurrence that inflamed animosity. The Indians finally capitulated and a fragile harmony was created between the Indians and Spaniards.[15]

Don Cristóbal Baca's descendents fled to El Paso with the rest of the Spaniards during the Pueblo Revolt. Based upon timeframe assumptions it was Captain Cristóbal's grandson, Cristóbal Baca II and his family and other relatives, who fled to El Paso. Cristóbal Baca II would have died in El Paso during the Pueblo Revolt, but his family, probably his son, Manuel, returned to New Mexico with de Vargas. They resettled in Bernalillo, north of the Albuquerque area, rather than returning to Santa Fe. Elfego's ancestors chose the more central area of the Rio Grande river valley to settle. It is believed some of the extended Baca family remained in the El Paso area, because relatives of Elfego Baca are known to have been residing in the El Paso area in the 1800s.

A New Nation — Mexico

Mexico was born out of New Spain after the first rebellion against the current government system began in 1810. The heavy-handed government of the Gachupínes for the last 300 years and the rise of the mestizo class of peoples was on a collision course in history.

The revolution was started by a priest named Miguel Hidalgo y Costilla. Miguel Hidalgo, an educated *Criollo,* was a fifty-seven year old parish priest in Dolores, a poor Indian village about one hundred miles northwest of Mexico City. Hidalgo's liberal ideas included giving equal rights to Indians and *mestizos,* along with ending the governmental grip of the *Gachupínes* over New Spain.

A Jesuit priest, Hidalgo was incensed by the poverty and exploitation of the natives and *mestizos.* An educated man, Hidalgo became increasingly interested in commerce and his humanitarian efforts. At this time in New Spain it was illegal to manufacture any goods and all merchandise goods had to be purchased and imported from Spain.

Hidalgo used his house as a night school for artisans and started a factory for making pottery and another for curing leather. He grew mulberry trees for the nourishment of silkworms, cultivated olive groves, and grew vineyards for wine making. He created workshops and taught the locals skills of carpentry, blacksmithing, and wool weaving. These commercial activities were illegal in New Spain and teaching Indians and *mestizos* skilled trades violated Spanish law.

Hidalgo's political beliefs were also fed by intellectual societies which had sprung up in the early 19th century. When Napoleon invaded Spain and took the Spanish crown in 1808 strife in New Spain intensified.

A young military captain, Ignacio José de Allende y Unzaga, shared Hidalgo's beliefs. He became Hidalgo's co-conspirator in the beginning of this war for independence from Spain. On the morning of September 16, 1810, Father Hidalgo held mass and gave what is known as the *'Grito de Dolores.'* It was a call to the people to leave their homes and join him against the viceroy and the government. Hidalgo's main reason for the revolt was the prevalent social stratification of the poor. Not unlike the Spaniards fighting the Moors, the peasants dropped their plows, left their homes, and went to war.

¡*Muerte a los Gachupínes!* (Death to the Gachupínes!) was the rallying cry from the rebels who followed Hidalgo. His army led by himself and Allende began with eight hundred men, about half on horseback. They declared independence and marched on to Guanajuato, a major colonial mining center governed by Spaniards (*Gachupínes* and *Criollos*). The rebel army grew as more Indians and *mestizos* joined the march freeing towns along the way.

They fought and won many battles, but were unable to defeat the main Spanish army in Mexico City. Hidalgo was defeated, captured and executed, yet, the execution of Hidalgo did not deter the Mexicans to fight for their freedom. Hidalgo's cry for independence has become the emblem of Mexico's struggle for independence and is celebrated as Mexican Independence Day, September 16th, each year. One man, a *Criollo,* a Spaniard born in the New World, had the courage to challenge the Spanish Empire with his life and for the freedom of others.

Hidalgo carried a banner with the image of *la Virgen de Guadalupe* (Our Lady of Guadalupe) to comfort his people. Like Cortés' *conquistadores* who prayed to Santiago, their War Saint, the image of *la Virgen de*

Guadalupe gave Hidalgo's people hope and strength in the face of great danger and was visibly their protection.

Elfego Baca, like Hidalgo, saw injustice and rose against it, displaying raw courage against unbelievable odds. He and the statue of *Nuestra Señora Santa Ana* (Our Lady of Saint Anne) held off a mob of eighty Texas cowboys for thirty-six hours.

Hidalgo was followed by other peasant leaders, such as José María Morelos y Pavón, Mariano Matamoros, and Vicente Guerrero, who all led armies of native and racially mixed revolutionaries against the Spanish and the Royalists.

Author's Note: Royalists were mostly *Criollos* who supported the Spanish crown's authority in New Spain.

The push for Mexican independence was further exacerbated by unrest and war in Spain. Napoleon's invasion of Spain and the continuing war with France caused major economic devastation to Spain and New Spain. King Ferdinand VII of Spain abdicated and Napoleon placed his own brother on the throne of Spain. Napoleon's rule in Spain brought a more liberal government and in 1812 a new Constitution was drafted for Spain. One of the more hotly debated portions of the Constitution gave rights to *mestizos* in Mexico and other mixed-race persons throughout the Spanish Empire. These rights included voting and equality rights, thus removing the feudal system currently in place throughout New Spain. These liberal ideas infuriated the Royalists and ruling class of Mexico forcing them into action.

Ironically, it was the Royalists, mostly *Criollos*, who ultimately brought about independence to Mexico. In response to the Constitution of 1812, Mexican Royalists supported the call for independence as a means of maintaining their privileged position in Mexican society.

In early 1821, Agustín de Iturbide, the leader of the Royalist forces negotiated the Plan of Iguala with Vicente Guerrero. The result was the Treaty of Córdoba, which recognized Mexican independence and formed the country of Mexico. Under the plan, Mexico was to be established as an independent constitutional monarchy, the privileged position of the Catholic Church would be maintained, and *Criollos* of Spanish descent would be regarded as equal to *Gachupines*. Mexicans of mixed or pure Indian blood would have lesser rights. The rights for the *mestizos,* for which Hidalgo gave his life, were still not equal when the new country of Mexico emerged.

Many challenges faced the infant country of Mexico. The economy needed to be revitalized and large armies with their leaders needed to be demobilized to insure that any one of them would not start another revolt. Hundreds of thousands of people had died and social dislocation caused by the War of Independence needed healing. In this chaotic environment, Mexico tried to forge a new nation out of great instability and the transformation was difficult and painful. Mexico inherited a vast empire that stretched north to California and what is now the American Southwest and extended south to Panama. Some of the Central American territories rebelled against Mexican rule during the early growth of the new nation and the army was mustered to smother the revolts.

For the next thirty years, Mexico was deeply divided and had over forty governments. Most of them were military coups paid in blood. General Antonio López de Santa Anna presided over eleven of them, as the country's *caudillo*, or leader, mostly with an iron fist. Santa Anna, a wealthy *Criollo* landowner, wielded great power over the fledgling country. From his hacienda in Veracruz he would set out with motley armies, alternately sparking or putting down uprisings, frequently accepting the invitation to become President, only to resign or be overthrown months later. A skillful general and then politician, he flip-flopped his positions on the government style in Mexico several times in an opportunistic manner. Republic, monarchy, military, or dictatorship, Mexico suffered through all forms of government during these formative years by Santa Anna and the numerous other dictators, *caudillos*, and military leaders. The inability to form a stable government in Mexico led to turmoil and war with the United States.

Image of General Antonio López de Santa Anna from the 1852 book Historia de Mejico by Don Lucas Alaman.

Santa Anna was hardly the only leader of the fractured new nation of Mexico. However, he is most remembered by many historians for his failures. The most epic failure — the loss of the northern territories to the United States, starting with Texas.

The Texas Rebellion

The Spanish Province of Texas was sparsely inhabited in the early 1800s. The history of Texas is quite different than the history of New Mexico, although the territories are quite close in proximity. While the push into New Mexico was for GOLD, the push into Texas was for LAND. Remote from the central Spanish government, cut off from many of the trade routes, most Spanish settlers did not inhabit this barren province voluntarily.

It is estimated the total Spanish population of Texas in 1820 was around 4000. Things were about to change in the next twenty years. The history of Texas is tightly intertwined with the political changes happening in New Spain, as the nation of Mexico was emerging in the 1820s. It was in New Spain's and later Mexico's best interest to colonize the vast northern territories with citizens loyal to Mexico City.

Moses Austin was a Connecticut-born entrepreneur working in Virginia and engaged in the lead mining business. With his lead mine playing out, he heard about rich lead mines under Spanish controlled regions of the west. After obtaining permission from the Spanish government in New Spain, he and his party of miners and slaves headed for Missouri. Austin was granted a square league of land, about 4,428 acres, on which he found lead deposits. He created the first permanent settlement in Washington County, Missouri. He started a lead mine, built a smelter, and built a new town on the property granted by the Spanish Crown. At this time, this part of Missouri was included in the territories of New Spain. The mine turned a profit for about ten years, before the economy collapsed after the War of 1812. The lead market went dry and he went bankrupt.

Austin needed a way to recoup his losses. In 1820 and eight hundred miles later, he entered San Antonio de Bexar, in the Spanish Province of Texas. He tried to use his experience with the Spanish royalty to convince them to allow him to establish an American colony, but was refused. By a lucky coincidence he met up with an old friend, Felipe Enrique Neri, known in Texas as Baron de Bastrop. With Bastrop's help Austin was able to obtain permission to settle up to three hundred families in Texas. On January 17, 1821, Moses Austin's Texas land grant was given by the Spanish Provincial Viceroy Apodaca and was later renewed by the newly created Mexican government, which took control of Mexico with the Treaty of Córdoba on August 24, 1821.

Fernando Orozco Linares in his book *Historia de México* writes about the reasons and advantages of colonization to Mexico:

> Translation:
> As Texas was territory unknown and abandoned, Mexico wanted to colonize it with foreigners, whom only it was asked to be Catholics. Viceroy Apodaca had given permission to the Anglo-American Moses Austin to establish a colony of 300 families in Texas, permission which passed to his son Stephen in 1823. With federalism was created the State of Coahuila, which had annexed the province of Texas and agreed to allow all kinds of foreigners, giving them land and many agricultural and industrial franchise because they could buy in the

United States machinery for planting and growing cotton, which they sold to the British at a great price.[16]

After receiving authorization to colonize, Moses Austin began organizing his first colony, however he became ill and died on his last trip back to Texas with the first of the American colonists. According to his agreement with the Viceroy Apodaca, his son Stephen Fuller Austin inherited the task of completing the arrangements for Austin's Texas colony. Steven Austin selected the lower reaches of the Colorado and Brazos Rivers as the site for the colony. According to Henderson K. Yoakum in his book *History of Texas from Its First Settlement in 1685 to Its Annexation by the United States in 1846,* the first colonists began arriving in December 1821. Fernando Orozco Linares wrote in *Historia de México* that it was 1823. The date is less important than the influx of colonists. After independence was won from Spain, Mexico continued colonization of Texas:

> In 1824, the Mexican government, which owned Texas, began to actively encourage the American colonization of Texas in order to promote trade and development. By 1830, about 7,000 Americans lived in Texas, outnumbering Hispanic settlers two to one. The Mexican government gave large land grants to agents, called empresarios [sic], who contracted to travel East to recruit settlers. Many of these empresarios were widely successful, and some, like Stephen F. Austin, the most

successful of all, gained great influence both with the Mexican government and the Texan settlers.[17]

Thus the Anglo-American colonization of Texas began. These new settlers were to be industrious and otherwise hard-working, Catholic, and willing to become Mexican citizens in exchange for land grants. Most all immigrants were hard-working, but the latter two criteria were not easily enforced and would later harbor resentments against the Mexican government:

> Anglo-Americans were attracted to Hispanic Texas because of inexpensive land. Undeveloped land in the United States land offices cost $1.25 an acre for a minimum of 80 acres ($100) payable in specie [coin] at the time of purchase. In Texas each head of a family, male or female, could claim a headright [sic] of 4,605 acres (one league — 4,428 acres of grazing land and one labor — 177 acres of irrigable farm land) at a cost about four cents an acre ($184) payable in six years, a sum later reduced by state authorities.[18]

After his father's death, Stephen Austin and other colonizers brought nearly 25,000 people into Texas, most of them Anglo-Americans. These colonists were obviously more loyal to the United States than to Mexico. This is understandable since they came from the United States, where they were protected by the U.S. Constitution. Since Mexico declared and fought for its independence from

Spain only a few years earlier, it was a new country with ambitious leaders, and still in political disorder. Mexico's government struggled in its early years of independence to find a solid form of government. It would not be until somewhat later when General Santa Anna would unite Mexico.

Amongst these new Anglo-American colonists was Sam Houston. Houston was born in Virginia, raised in the mountains of East Tennessee, and was once governor of Tennessee. Before Sam Houston even set foot in Texas, it was rumored he had high ambitions toward conquering Texas for the United States. President Andrew Jackson was not amused and at first wanted no part in such a plan. This is quite clear from the following letter from President Jackson to Sam Houston on June 21, 1829:

> "It has been communicated to me," said he, "that you had the illegal enterprise in view of conquering Texas; that you had declared you would, in less than two years, be emperor of that country, by conquest. I must have really thought you deranged to have believed you had such a wild scheme in contemplation; and particularly, when it was communicated that the physical force to be employed was the Cherokee Indians! Indeed, my dear sir, I can not [sic] believe you have any such chimerical, visionary scheme in view. Your pledge of honor to the contrary is a sufficient guaranty that you will never engage in any enterprise injurious to

your country, or that would tarnish your fame."[19]

Despite Jackson's admonishment, Sam Houston did not give up his dream of conquering Texas. Between the letter from Jackson in 1829 and 1832, Sam Houston married Eliza Allen, although she left him shortly after the marriage. This was a great embarrassment to him and prompted him to resign as governor of Tennessee. Afterward he had several mistresses and wives and lived for some time in the Cherokee Indian Nation in Oklahoma. To say his life was colorful, for the times, would be an understatement. In 1832 Houston once again became enamored with Texas. After arriving in Texas, he quickly became engaged in the political events which would finally shape Texas into a state.

Sam Houston wrote to President Andrew Jackson of the situation in the Mexican Province of Texas. In the letter he states the desire of the leaders of Texas to join the United States, and also reports on the unstable Mexican government. Antonio López de Santa Anna was at the root of the unrest and it was rumored he, Santa Anna, wanted to start a civil war in Mexico. In other words, Houston believed Texas was 'ripe for the picking.'

General Sam Houston wrote a passionate letter to President Andrew Jackson, from Natchitoches, Louisiana, February 13, 1833:

> Dear Sir: Having been as far as Bexar, in the province of Texas, where I had an interview with the Camanche [sic] Indians, I am in possession of some information that will doubtless be interesting to you, and may be calculated to forward your views, if you

should entertain any, touching the acquisition of Texas by the United States. That such a measure is desirable by nineteen twentieths of the population of the province, I can not [sic] doubt. They are now without laws to govern or protect them. Mexico is involved in civil war. The federal constitution has never been in operation. The government is essentially despotic, and must be so for years to come. The rulers have not honesty, and the people have not intelligence.

The people of Texas are determined to form a state government, and to separate from Coahuila; and, unless Mexico is soon restored to order, and the constitution revived and re-enacted, the province of Texas will remain separate from the confederacy of Mexico. She has already beaten and expelled all the troops of Mexico from her soil, nor will she permit them to return. She can defend herself against the whole power of Mexico; for really Mexico is powerless and penniless to all intents and purposes. Her want of money, taken in connection with the course which Texas must and will adopt, will render a transfer of Texas inevitable to some power; and if the United States does not press for it, England will most assuredly obtain it by some means. Now is a very important crisis for Texas, as relates to her future prosperity and safety, as well as the relation it is to bear toward the United States. If Texas is desirable to the United States, it is now in the most favorable attitude, perhaps, that it can be, to obtain it on fair terms. England is pressing her suit for it, but its citizens will resist if any transfer should be made of them to any other power but the United States.

I have travelled nearly five hundred miles across Texas, and am now enabled to judge pretty correctly of the soil and the resources of the country. And I have no hesitation in pronouncing it the finest country, to its extent, upon the globe; for, the greater portion of it is richer and more healthy, in my opinion, than West Tennessee. There can be no doubt but the country east of the Rio Grande would sustain a population of ten millions of souls. My opinion is, that Texas will, by her members in convention on the first of April, declare all that country as Texas proper, and form a state constitution. I expect to be present at the convention, and will apprise you of the course adopted so soon as its members have taken a final action. It is probable I may make Texas my abiding-place: in adopting this course, I will never forget the country of my birth.

From this point I will notify the commissioners of the Indians, at Fort Gibson, of my success, which will reach you through the war department.

I have with much pride and inexpressible satisfaction seen your messages and PROCLAMATION touching the nullifiers of the south and their "peaceable remedies." God grant that you may save the Union! It does seem to me that it is reserved for you, and you alone, to render millions so great a blessing. I hear all voices commend your course, even in Texas — where is felt the liveliest interest for the preservation of the republic.

Permit me to tender you my sincere felicitations, and most earnest solicitude for your health and happiness — and your future glory, connected with the prosperity of the Union.

    Your friend and obedient servant,
    Sam Houston[20]

Sam Houston was a military man achieving the rank of General. His aspirations in life involved mostly war and power. It was therefore likely he saw Texas as a huge opportunity for the United States and mostly for himself. In his letter he portrays the Mexican government as both tyrannical and dishonest. He thought the Mexican people were not intelligent, a typical attitude of superiority and a sentiment which many Anglo-Texans shared:

> Between 1821 and 1835, the population of non-Indian Texas expanded to between 35,000 and 50,000. Most new settlers were Anglo-Americans who often brought their prejudices against Mexico with them, whether they were from the North or the South. Many disliked Mexican culture, Mexican folkways, Mexican justice — and the Protestants among them resented the omnipresence of the Roman Catholic Church. All of these Anglo-American settlers had ties to the US, and many undoubtedly longed for the time when they would live under the American flag again. The ineptitude of the Mexican government made the situation even worse. In 1826, Hayden Edwards organized the Republic of Fredonia and tried to drive the Mexicans from East Texas, but in the end, he had to flee the province himself. Troubled by the rising spirit of rebellion, the Mexican Congress enacted the Law of 1830, which forbade most immigration and imposed duties on all imports. Anglo-Americans in Texas responded with the same anger that New Englanders had once shown when Britain imposed tax restrictions on the original American colonies.[21]

The new settlers trekked to Texas with the lure of free land quickly outnumbering the Mexicans living in the state. They exhibited little interest in the Mexican culture. One family of these early Texas settlers were the Slaughters from Louisiana. Early in 1830 William Slaughter moved his family to Texas, including his adult son George. Like many others, William looked at Texas for new opportunities, bigger and better land, and a better life for his family. William would live to see this dream, but would not live to see his grandson, John, become a Texas cattle baron. Fifty years after his grandfather moved to Texas, John Slaughter and his cowboys would continue to move west into the peaceful New Mexican valley of the San Francisco River and confront Elfego Baca:

> Like many of the new settlers, William and George Slaughter would be supportive and become active in the movements to liberate Texas from Mexican rule. George Slaughter served as a courier under Sam Houston and is credited with delivering a message to William B. Travis at the Alamo.[22]

Fernando Orozco Linares in his book *Historia de México* writes about how Mexico saw the rebellion of the distant Province of Texas:

> Translation:
> In Texas, there had formed a large and active population divided into three focus groups: the annexation, in favor of joining the United States, the independent party separate from Mexico to form an independent nation, and the

Mexican, who asked to continue to be united to Mexico, as a federal state. The Mexican government was misbehaving with the settlers: high tariffs made it impossible for American machinery to be imported as Mexico did not produce any kind of machinery, the Texan territory was under military rule, and the commanders abused their authority, at the same time the Mexican soldiers were committing robberies and all kinds of excesses. Furthermore, they were neglected by the government of Coahuila, which they depended on as it did not accept any representation or complaint, nor had their obituaries, neither judges, or schools nor were they defended from savage Indians.

However, as mentioned above, the immediate cause of the rebellion or separation of the Texans was to abolish the federal system and the establishment of centralism. The settlers gathered in San Felipe de Austin to organize, in May 1833 and two years later had a second convention in Nacogdoches, on November 7, 1835, tentatively declaring its independence because Santa Anna had broken the federal pact. The Texans wasted no time; they were well armed and had received the support of many American volunteers, so they attacked the small garrison of San Antonio de Velasco, forcing them to surrender. With the ease of the victory they felt good about owning Texas. In New Washington they formally signed the minutes of its independence on March 2, 1836, constituting of a republic with Sam Houston as president and Lorenzo de Zavala as Vice President, then set out to buy weapons, equipment, ammunition, and recruiting volunteers in the United States because they knew that Mexico would want to punish them.[23]

In September of 1835, when all political solutions between the Province of Texas and Mexico City were exhausted, small skirmishes between Texas volunteers and Mexican forces erupted. By October of the same year, the Texas rebellion was in full force:

> Expresses and circulars were sent everywhere, to raise volunteers. The object, "to take Bexar, and drive the Mexican soldiery out of Texas," was boldly announced at San Felipe, and repeated by every committee of safety in the country.[24]

The Texas colonists escalated the rebellion in the fall of 1835 driving all Mexican troops from Mexican Texas. After all, it was barely sixty years since the patriots had declared independence from England and their descendents were hardly likely to accept foreign rule. The Anglo-Americans in Texas were bound and determined to be free from Mexico's tax demands and took advantage of Mexico's instability to fight for Texas' freedom and prevailed.

In 1836 the Mexican Province of Texas declared independence from Mexico and formed the Republic of Texas. General Santa Anna marched north to bring Texas back under Mexican control. He succeeded by using merciless force, however the Texas campaign posed enormous challenges to logistics, manpower, and support. Santa Anna forced wealthy Mexican families to fund the Texas campaign while he recruited ex-convicts, derelicts, and Indians to his army.

His first attempt to retake Texas ended in disaster with the Texans pushing his forces back. His soldiers were untrained and undisciplined and the Indians spoke no Spanish and could not understand military commands. His motley army struggled with the cold weather, food shortages, and disease, but Santa Anna seemed oblivious to their condition. Confident, he arrogantly rallied his troops to attack the Mission in San Antonio called the Alamo.

Approximately 100 Texans were garrisoned at the Alamo. It was winter and moving supplies, cannon, and men was difficult for the Texans. Sam Houston sent James 'Jim' Bowie to demolish the Alamo and move the garrison, but Bowie believed the Mission to be strategic to the Texas cause.

Santa Anna gathered about 6,000 Mexican soldiers and marched to Texas with the goal of taking San Antonio, culminating with the Battle of the Alamo from February 23 to March 6, 1836. Santa Anna's army killed all of the Texans at the Alamo, reclaimed San Antonio for Mexico, however, he also incurred heavy losses. Santa Anna took no prisoners and ordered the execution of both combatants and civilians — about 350 innocent men, women, and children. He showed no mercy to the Texans, an act which rubbed the Texans raw for future generations, giving them the war cry 'Remember the Alamo.'

After his victory at the Alamo, Santa Anna still having superior numbers of troops pursued Sam Houston's beleaguered Texas army east, catching up to him near the San Jacinto River.

In a bold move in the middle of the afternoon of April 21, 1836, Sam Houston attacked, while Santa Anna's troops were resting and setting up camp. This bold and unorthodox battle technique caught the Mexican army by surprise and the Texans won the Battle of San Jacinto, defeating Santa Anna's army. The war was over.

Author's Note: The preceding narrative is only small snippets of all the political arguments and battles between Texas and Mexico, resulting in the Texas Declaration of Independence of 1836. As history proves though, often one man, one event, or one decision can change the course of history.

Before and after the war between Texans and Mexico, William and George Slaughter and the family thrived in Texas, first in the Provincial Territory of Texas, and later in the Republic of Texas. Much like the Spanish *conquistadores* heading to New Spain, these American colonists were looking for riches. This time it was not GOLD, it was LAND.

Author's Note: Interestingly, the 'black gold' of Texas oil would not be discovered for many years.

Land was cheap and land was plentiful, but life was hard on the Texas plains where colonists had to fight both Indians and Mexicans. After the independence of Texas, the new land owners, such as the Slaughters, began ranching and running large herds of cattle freely over the lush Texas prairie.

George's son, John, would grow up on this Texas prairie after Texas won independence from Mexico, learning the cattle business from the saddle. John and his brother would push further west into the panhandle of Texas, before then pushing into New Mexico to find land and markets for their cows. Their push into New Mexico would finally push their ranch cowboys into a confrontation with one man, Elfego Baca.

Immigrants to Texas were not limited to American citizens. New immigrants from Ireland, Germany, Poland, and other European countries made their way to Texas and Oklahoma. The mix of these international immigrants added interest to the culture of Texas. Cotton farming and ranching dominated the economics of the land.

Southern cotton farmers brought their slaves to Texas. The Mexican government had not allow slavery and many slaves were listed as 'indentured servants.' Later the slavery issue would again split Texas as the United States engaged in the Civil War and Texas joined the Confederacy.

James K. Polk was elected president of the United States, as a Democrat, in 1844. The Democrats' platform supported and included an idea called 'manifest destiny.'

In 1845, newspaper editor John Louis O'Sullivan coined the term 'manifest destiny' in the July – August issue of the *United States Magazine and Democratic Review*. The article proclaimed:

> ". . . our manifest destiny to overspread the continent allotted by Providence for the free development of our multiplying millions."

The annexation of Texas was the subject of the article by O'Sullivan and became a mantra for pro-expansionists in general. He continued in a second article:

> ". . . and that claim is by the right of our manifest destiny to overspread and to possess the whole of the continent which Providence has given us for the development of the great experiment of liberty and federated self-government entrusted to us."

The Democrats pushed the idea of manifest destiny, stating Americans were predestined to occupy the entire North American continent, thereby giving them the predestined right to continue annexing land. The Republic of Texas was annexed in 1845. President Polk wanted to claim New Mexico, California, and some disputed land on the southern Texas border with Mexico. Mexico had already lost Texas and did not plan to lose more of its land.

President Polk was so resolute in acquiring the land that on January of 1846 he sent American troops to the southern border of Texas, to provoke Mexico into war. On April 25, 1846, Mexican and American troops engaged in several skirmishes, some military troops from both sides were killed. This was the excuse President Polk was looking for. He declared to the American people, "Mexico has invaded our territory and shed American blood upon American soil." He sent the order to declare war against Mexico to Congress on May 11, 1846.

U. S. forces captured and occupied Texas, Santa Fe, and Los Angeles. In 1847 General Zachary Taylor marched south from Texas defeating the Mexican army commanded by General Santa Anna, while in the meantime General Winfield Scott landed in Veracruz and advanced toward the capital. By September of that year, Scott took Mexico City and raised the American flag above the National Palace.

The advent of losing the Mexican-American War forced the Mexican government to begin negotiating the Treaty of Guadalupe Hidalgo to transfer a large portion of the northern Mexican territories to the United States.

While the Treaty of Guadalupe Hidalgo was being negotiated, some in Congress warned against annexing some or all of the Mexican territories. John C. Calhoun, Senator of South Carolina, warned that admitting Mexicans into the Union would diminish the racial order of the United States. His statement on the floor of the senate protests against the annexation of Texas over racial issues:

> "I know further, sir, that we have never dreamt of incorporating into our Union any but the Caucasian race — the free white race. To incorporate Mexico, would be the very first instance of the kind of incorporating an Indian race; for more than half of the Mexicans are Indians, and the other is composed chiefly of mixed tribes. I protest against such a union as that! Ours, sir, is the Government of a white race. The greatest misfortunes of Spanish America are to be traced to the fatal error of placing these colored races on an equality with the white race. That error destroyed the social arrangement which formed the basis of society. The Portuguese and ourselves have escaped

> — the Portuguese at least to some extent — and we are the only people on this continent which have made revolutions without being followed by anarchy. And yet it is professed and talked about to erect these Mexicans into a Territorial Government, and place them on an equality with the people of the United States. I protest utterly against such a project."

This statement by the senator from a southern state sums up the feelings of many of the Anglo-Texans. Most of the original Texas colonists originated from the south, and Texas sympathized with the south, and became a confederate state during the American Civil War.

Senator Calhoun continued his discourse against annexation of Texas and demeaned the intelligence of the "impure race":

> "But, Mr. President, suppose all these difficulties removed; suppose these people attached to our Union, and desirous of incorporating with us, ought we to bring them in? Are they fit to be connected with us? Are they fit for self-government and for governing you? Are you, any of you, willing that your States should be governed by these twenty-odd Mexican States, with a population of about only one million of your blood, and two or three millions of mixed blood, better informed, all the rest pure Indians, a mixed blood equally ignorant

and unfit for liberty, impure races, not as good as Cherokees or Choctaws?"

While Calhoun made these statements about Hispanics, it had likewise been said by Spanish politicians in New Spain in regards to Anglo-Americans. When Moses Austin was allowed to colonize Texas, it was feared the newcomers would never be loyal to New Spain and the Spanish Crown.

On February 2, 1848, in exchange for $15 million, the Mexican government signed the Treaty of Guadalupe Hidalgo and surrendered large portions of land, which included California, Arizona, and New Mexico as well as Texas to the United States. Soon afterwards American troops withdrew from Mexico City, leaving a mutilated nation in danger of even greater disintegration. Santa Anna's loss of Texas culminated in the loss of approximately one half of all the Mexican territory to the United States.

After Texas was admitted as the 28th state, the Texas land grab began anew by Anglos, both those already living in Texas and new settlers. Except for the elite Hispanic families many Spanish land grants were taken from smaller *ranchos*, either because the families had lost their documents or couldn't afford to pay the taxes. Even though the Treaty of Guadalupe Hidalgo had provisions to protect the original Spanish landowners, new laws were used to the advantage of the Anglos to acquire the land grants at an extremely reduced rate or by force.

The Homestead Act of 1862 enticed many pioneers to the west with essentially free land. The land grab escalated in states such as Texas, Oklahoma, Kansas, New Mexico, and further west. With land claims from Spain neither marked nor filed with the American government, land was land. It did not matter who owned it, unless it was protected by guns.

When Texas became a state, the Slaughters received generous land grants on which they began their cattle business. To the victor goes the spoils. In Texas, many Hispanic landowners lost their land and rights and Anglo ranchers, such as the Slaughters, became the 'rightful' owners.

Not just land disputes created animosity during the mid 1800s. Hispanic-Texans, *Tejanos*, along with Mexican citizens created a good business hauling food and merchandise from the Texas port of Indianola to San Antonio and other towns by oxcart. They were attacked by masked Anglo-Texan competitors destroying the oxcarts, stealing the freight, and killing and wounding the *Tejano* carters. Attacks on *Tejano* carters was reported near Seguin in 1855, and by July of 1857 the violence on the carters increased substantially. The so-called 'Cart War' was ethnic and racially motivated, but received little help from the law. There was no serious effort by local authorities to apprehend the Anglo-Texan criminals, which only emboldened them to create more violence against the carters. *Tejanos* believed a 'campaign of death' against them and Mexican traders was under way in Texas.

Animosity between Anglo-Texans and Hispanic-Texans was inevitable after the fall of the Alamo and the war between the United States and Mexico. Although the Treaty of Guadalupe Hidalgo guaranteed those of Spanish descent who stayed in Texas full citizenship, they were still considered undesirable and unwelcome on their own land. The Anglo-Texans and their 'Remember the Alamo' mantra would often make life miserable for the Hispanic-Texans, and would extend to Hispanics all over the Southwest. It affected the peaceful Hispanic villagers of the San Francisco valley in New Mexico when the rowdy

Texas cowboys felt justified to harass them, until one Hispanic, Elfego Baca, stood his ground.

New Mexico Territory

New Mexico remained under Spanish rule until the Mexican revolution in the 1820s. Although New Spain was in turmoil with revolution, the settlements to the north, New Mexico and Arizona, were not directly involved since there was minimal contact with the government in New Spain. These northern settlements were developing more or less independently.

After Mexico won independence from Spain, the Santa Fe Trail was opened in 1822 connecting Santa Fe, New Mexico, with markets from the United States and Santa Fe thrived. Missouri merchants sent manufactured goods to Santa Fe and furs and other Mexican or Indian goods were sent to Missouri. Santa Fe transformed from an old Spanish settlement to a place of commerce.

In 1821, the year Mexico declared independence from Spain, over 20,000 people resided in New Mexico mostly of Spanish decent. By comparison, only about 4,000 resided in Texas at the same time, but Texas was growing fast and the western land push was in full force.

In 1841 New Mexico's Governor was informed by authorities from Mexico about an expedition of three hundred soldiers from the Republic of Texas headed to Santa Fe. The Texans were intent on taking the New Mexico Territory away from Mexico. Mexico, still upset from losing Texas, kept a close eye on the movements of the Texas army, supplying New Mexico Governor Armijo with arms and materials to repel the invasion:

> Armijo met them with a large force of well-armed soldiers, and quickly they were persuaded to surrender, a cause for much rejoicing throughout the

> territory. Armijo sent the Texans, under guard, on the long journey to Mexico City and then on to Veracruz. Most of the Texans were incarcerated in the Perote prison until the United States government negotiated their release.[25]

While the war between Mexico and the United States was in progress, little happened in New Mexico until June 1846, when General Kearney marched into the undefended northern Mexican territory. Governor Armijo did not have the troops and arms to oppose Kearny, thus allowing him to march into Las Vegas. From the roof of a building in the plaza, Kearny announced the following:

> "I have come amongst you by orders of my government, to take possession of your country and extend over it the laws of the United States . . ."[26]

This was reminiscent of what Hernando Cortés told Montezuma and his Aztec people when he marched into Tenochtitlán, now Mexico City. General Kearny marched into Santa Fe on August 18, 1846, ending two and a half centuries of Spanish and Mexican rule without firing one single shot. He made the following statement to the people of Santa Fe and again it parallels what Hernando Cortés told the Aztecs:

> "To better your condition and make you part of the Republic of the United States. We mean not to murder you or rob you of your property. Your families shall be free from molestation; your women secure from violence. My soldiers shall

take nothing from you but what they pay for — we do not mean to take away your religion — I do hereby proclaim that you are no longer Mexican subjects; you are now become American citizens . . ."[27]

In one last view on why the United States coveted the northern territories of Mexico, Benjamin M. Read in his book *Guerra Mexico-Americana* states, aside from President Polk's manifest destiny, there was a racial element on the side of the United States. In his book he argues there was racial tension between the Anglo-Saxon and Latin races, which dated back to 1819 when Spain lost Florida to the United States.

Benjamin Maurice Read was a self-taught historian, who was proud of his mother's Spanish culture. Raised and educated in Santa Fe, he was a teacher, lawyer, and territorial legislator. His passion was history and he wrote frequent articles in local Spanish-language newspapers:

> The subject of his writing was often the way Nuevomexicanos were unjustly denigrated in the Eastern press and not treated as equal citizens of the territory. A bilingual man, Read had an appreciation of the power of the written word to establish authority in Anglo society, and considered himself a mediator between the two cultures. Although he was a great admirer of United States institutions of government, he also had a deep respect for the accomplishments of his Hispano forbearers.[28]

When General Kearny raised the American flag in Santa Fe in 1846, Elfego's grandfather Jose Miguel Baca was operating a merchandising store in Socorro, New Mexico, along the King's Highway, known as El Camino Real. Elfego's ancestors had been living in New Mexico for over two hundred years. His father, Francisco, was about eleven when Kearny took control of Santa Fe. In Texas, John Slaughter's father, George, was running cattle on the open plains. The next forty years would bring immense changes to both states and to the families they supported, and would bring these two specific families, Baca and Slaughter, both change and conflict.

When the Civil War broke out, New Mexico and Texas would view the struggle differently over the next decade. After the Civil War, in 1874, New Mexico Territorial delegate Stephen B. Elkins read a thirty page speech to Congress, making an argument that New Mexico should be allowed to join the Union, based on the promises in the Treaty of Guadalupe Hidalgo. Following the speech by Elkins, the proposed bill for New Mexico's entry into the Union gained much support. It passed both the House and Senate, but didn't pass congressional reconciliation. The forty-second session of Congress adjourned without compromise. New Mexico remained a territory.

Elkins was a tenacious man and in 1876 he convinced the Committee of the Territories to support another statehood bill for New Mexico, except this time there was racist opposition in the Congress. In John M. Nieto-Phillips book, *The Language of Blood, The Making of Spanish-American Identity in New Mexico, 1880s – 1930s*, he interprets the fifteen-page minority report against the new statehood bill:

> . . . opponents argued that New Mexico possessed neither the "population,

industry, intelligence, [nor the] wealth to entitle this Territory to admission in the Union as a sovereign state." Not only had New Mexico's demographic and economic growth been misrepresented, the minority report argued, but hostile relations between "the native population" and Indians had also drawn a dark cloud over all traces of "American" civilization in the region. New Mexico remained a forsaken territory, savage and undemocratic. Its people's "peculiar character" made it unworthy of self-government. The report further disparaged Nuevomexicanos for their lack of formal education, their deficiency in English, their fervent Catholicism, and most importantly, for their not possessing European or Anglo American ancestry or culture. It painted Nuevomexicanos as mixed-blood "Mexicans" of Spanish and Indian parentage, and possessing only the worst of both races: "Of the native population but few are pure-blood or Castilian, probably not more than fifty or one hundred families in all, the rest being a mixture of Spanish or Mexican and Indian in different degrees. With the decadence of early Spanish power and enterprise on this continent the inhabitants of this isolated region, with few exceptions, continued to sink, till now, for nigh two hundred years, into a condition of ignorance, superstition, and sloth that is unequaled by their Aztec neighbors, the Pueblo Indians."[29]

The political fight for New Mexico's statehood continued on in Congress for more than thirty years, mostly along racial lines. In no other situation would statehood be so long withheld. In 1882 Congress again debated statehood, adjourning without a vote. A champion of the cause was New Mexico's Chief Justice LeBaron Bradford Prince. He encouraged the citizens of New Mexico to be proud of their *conquistador* past. He wrote:

And as to the dignity which that name represents; New Mexico was never an ordinary province of New Spain, like the regions south of it. It was always a separate government, with authorities appointed directly by the Spanish King, and in all ancient documents it was called "The Kingdom of New Mexico."[30]

Chief Justice Prince, an Anglo, was an ardent statehood supporter and would come to be considered the 'Father of Statehood' to *Nuevomexicanos*. New Mexico finally became a state in 1912.

New Mexico has a rich and interesting history, both from the pueblo Indian perspective and the Spanish. The Baca family linage has been richly intertwined in the history of New Mexico for over two and a half centuries. Baca is still an old and well-respected Spanish surname in the area. Through strife, wars, and famine, one final thought can sum up this brief history of New Mexico — the BACA'S have survived!

San Francisco Valley, New Mexico, Territory

Nestled along the San Francisco and Tularosa rivers in western New Mexico, lush grasslands were home to the Apache Indians. Rocky escarpments and higher mountains, now named the Apache-Sitgreaves National Forest, surrounded peaceful valleys of irrigable land. Early New Mexican settlers generally homesteaded along the Rio Grande, running through the central part of the state.

By the 1800s Indian uprisings had been somewhat controlled and settlers began to look for greener pastures. Perfecto and Lucas Martinez, father and mother of Epitacio Martinez, were some of these New Mexican settlers. They and their family including their son, Epitacio, settled and survived in the San Francisco valley. Epitacio Martinez would continue to live there into adulthood and was the brave Hispanic man who attempted to save *el Burro* from being castrated by the Slaughter cowboys. Epitacio's bravery for attempting to intervene on behalf of *el Burro* has not made history as he deserves. The story of Epitacio's brush with death, at the hands of the Texas cowboys, catalysts the events which brought Elfego Baca to Frisco Plaza in the San Francisco valley in 1884. Henry Martinez, great-grandson of Epitacio, continues to live in the area today, now called Reserve, New Mexico. This is the story of his great-great-grandparents and their journey to the San Francisco valley.

Around the early 1800s in a village along the middle Rio Grande in New Mexico, between Socorro and Las Cruces, a small company of Spanish settlers chased a band of Apaches who had taken cattle and horses. The Spanish settlers overtook the Apaches about thirty miles west of the Rio Grande on a mesa above Alamosa Canyon. They killed most of the raiders and then rounded up the livestock before heading back to the village:

> These skirmishes were a common experience in New Mexico in the early 1800s, for no government had been able to protect the colonists from the Apaches. These Indians, who controlled the tangled mountain country west of the river, laughed at authorities. They said the only reason they let the Spanish stay on the Rio Grande was to raise cattle and corn. Then when the Indian needed food, he would go get it. So the tireless Apaches, with their deerskin clothing, high moccasins, and headbands around jet-black hair, were a dreaded sight to the settlers.[31]

Apaches on horseback. Photograph reproduction courtesy of the Socorro Historical Society.

Destined to Survive

While they searched for their livestock, a Spaniard named Martinez noticed there were no Apache bodies on the battlefield, and surmised the surviving warriors had gathered up the bodies and taken them up into the hills. Martinez kept a wary eye on the terrain for any sign of the enemy. In a bush not far from the battlefield, he spotted an Indian baby in a woven cradleboard. He was careful when he approached the bush, thinking it could be a trap.

What he found was no trap, but an Indian baby girl. Martinez wondered why the Apaches had abandoned the baby. Sometimes Apache women held the horses while the warriors were in battle. The Apache mother may have been scared, run away or was killed in the skirmish. Whatever the reason, Martinez would not leave the baby to the wolves and coyotes.

The Martinez's already had four sons. He decided to take the baby girl home and surprise his wife who had always wanted a girl in the family. The Martinez family was one of manthe early Spanish settlers in New Mexico, the northern province of New Spain. These people were adventurous and hardy in this land which was far away from their government. Viola M. Payne relates the story of the Martinez's life in the New Mexico frontier in her book *Three Angels Over Rancho Grande*, as told to her by Martinez family members:

> As Martinez rode home, he reflected on the sorry state of political affairs in New Mexico, this beautiful barbaric country which stirred memories of Spain. Many things about it he found desirable. The dry climate was fine for horses and cattle and sheep. Water could be ditched from the river for vineyards, grain, and alfalfa, just as in the homeland. Timber

grew in the mountains, and the hills above the river flowed bright with sunlight. When the rains came in July and August, with their towering clouds and shattered rainbows, the grass stirred like green waves in the wind. But it was no country for the weak and timid, for death lurked almost everywhere behind the beauty.

Martinez, like his fellow colonists from Spain, was a skilled artisan and farmer, with an inbred love of freedom and adventure. The colonists had gone almost beyond the reach of law here, yet had managed to setup a vestige of culture and civilization in their little villages. This was hardly surprising, since those chosen to go to land grants in New Mexico were men of good character, well trained in the Catholic faith. And they had clung to the faith in spite of their hardships. They had no Bibles to guide them, for the church provided their authority in religious matters. They could hope to see a priest only a few times each year, when some of the wagon supply trains came up from Chihuahua City, Mexico. These ox wagons brought travelers; and they also brought a scanty supply of food and tools, which cost the colonists plenty in sheep and cattle.

The Spanish had known how to handle many things about New Mexico. They had known what sort of houses to build — adobe, thick-walled, whitewashed, with heavy-beamed ceilings. These simple homes, with their fragrant little gardens, were grouped together for protection. However, after two hundred years of warfare, the Spanish could still not handle the Apache.

The recent overthrow of Spanish rule in Mexico had made political orphans of the New Mexico colonists without offering them any more protection from the Indians. The colonists always seemed to be caught in some power struggle beyond their control, and now they felt deserted by Spain. The Mexican government couldn't keep the Apache out of the state of Chihuahua, much less the far-flung Rio Grande valley! And the mountain kingdom of the Apache, including the Black Range, Gila, and Mogollon country — that land of thick evergreen forests, grama grass, foaming water, game, rich minerals — had hardly been touched by the Spanish explorers. When would this warfare ever end?[32]

Martinez returned home with the baby girl. Like her broad minded and tender hearted husband, Señora Martinez immediately fell in love with the small helpless Apache baby. She made a proper dress for the little girl and insisted the child be baptized and given a Christian name. They named her Sabastiana and the Martinez family welcomed the sweet, vulnerable baby into their arms and family.

The villagers however were distraught. How could the Martinez family raise an Indian, an Apache? It is understandable why these people who constantly battled the Apaches were prejudiced. To them Apaches were savages, not human. Señora Martinez rejected the gossip. She raised Sabastiana as she would her own daughter. The whole family loved Sabastiana, who was intelligent and sweet natured. This girl was no savage. As she grew up Sabastiana learned Spanish, learned to cook and sew, and knew only of her life in the Spanish village.

By the time Sabastiana turned eighteen most of the other girls were getting married, but Sabastiana had no suitors in this village. Her skin was a shade darker than the others and her hair dark and straight as it surrounded a beautiful face. She was Apache and the Spanish families in this small village were careful not to taint their purity of blood.

The Spanish customs of the time were very strict concerning daughters and marriage. They were protected until they became of age to marry, then the parents would choose a husband for the young woman. The Martinez family had a dilemma. Señora Martinez loved Sabastiana and didn't want the girl to leave her family or leave the village, so she resolved the problem by marrying Sabastiana to her son, Manuel.

According to family records, Manuel was happy to marry Sabastiana and in her he found a devoted and loving wife. They had several children including a boy they named Perfecto. Perfecto grew to be tall, broad shouldered, and his part-Apache skin a shade darker than his Spanish friends and neighbors along the river. In the tradition of his

Spanish ancestors, Perfecto learned how to manage cattle, sheep, and horses.

Perfecto fell in love with a beautiful young woman named Lucas Armijo and began courting her. The Armijo family owned the San Marcial Land Grant, one of the largest in the area. They were a pure-blooded Spanish family and relatives of the territorial governor, Manuel Armijo. As was the custom of Spanish families, they carefully planned their bloodlines. However, times were changing and the old Spanish customs could not be sustained in these rugged outposts. Lucas fell in love with Perfecto and wanted to marry him.

Lucas' older brother, Espedion, was adamantly opposed to the marriage stating, "it would be a disgrace for fair-skinned, blue-eyed Lucas to marry this big, dark, half-Apache fellow!"[33]

Lucas was a headstrong young woman who knew what she wanted and she wanted to marry Perfecto. The old ways were bending to new ways, born out of necessity and freedom. Lucas married Perfecto and their life together brought the Martinez family to the San Francisco valley.

Lucas Armijo de Martinez, mother of Epitacio Martinez. Photograph courtesy of the Martinez family.

In 1859 twelve Spanish families moved up the canyon of the Alamosa River, in central New Mexico, to the area of Monticello, then called Cañada Alamosa. There they planted vineyards and orchards and attempted to survive Apache attacks. Perfecto Martinez brought his family around this time hunting more grass for his cattle. The 1860 census lists Perfeto [Perfecto] as living in San Ygnacio de la Alamosa, Socorro, New Mexico Territory with his wife, Guadalupe [Lucas], sons Getacio [Epitacio] and Francisco, listed as 4 years and 3 years, respectively. Within a few years he and Lucas had four sons, Epitacio, Francisco, Tomas and Demecio, and two daughters, Panchita and Juanita.

Author's Note: Misspelling of names, particularly Spanish names, in documents, census information, and newspapers was typical, or the translation may alter accepted spelling, such as Getacio for Epitacio in the above census.

Cañada Alamosa or 'Canyon of the Cottonwoods,' now called Monticello northwest of Truth or Consequences, New Mexico, is a rich canyon where rain water drains out of the San Mateo Mountains toward the Rio Grande. Like ancient pueblo Indians many years prior, Hispanic farmers and ranchers began settling this lush area around 1856. It had warm springs just west of the Alamosa village. The settlers built their homes with adobe and arranged them around the plaza to protect the village from Apaches. Like the other settlers, Perfecto let his cattle roam on the escarpment of rocky terrain above the village and farmed food for his family in the valley.

Sometimes the Apaches would come to Alamosa and trade with the settlers and other times they would attack the outpost and take what they needed. There was no authority to protect the settlers from attacks in this lonely land. They had to find ways to protect themselves. For centuries, the Spanish people would drop their plows, close their shops, and pick up arms and fight the Moors. Here in New Mexico it was no different, but the fight was against the raiding Apaches.

When the United States signed the Treaty of Guadalupe Hidalgo with Mexico in 1848, and subsequently the Gadsden Purchase was ratified, the United States annexed this area into a United States territory making the residents, citizens. However, these governmental changes had little effect on the people living in the new territory — the land was still lush, the Apaches still attacked, and the winters were still cold.

The treaty had given the people of the New Mexico Territory a choice of leaving or staying under the new government. If they left, however, they would have to give up their land. The Martinez family, along with most others, were not willing to do that. And where would they go? They had no place to return to in Spain and the government of Mexico was uncertain. This was their home, their land, and had been for generations. Surely it would be better to take a chance under a democracy rather than to lose everything. Remote to the government, they hoped to continue to live their lives in peace, secluded and hidden by geography, in the valleys of New Mexico. Perhaps under the American government, with its forts and soldiers, they might even find some protection from the Apaches.

A few years later, the people of Cañada Alamosa had new problems when the American Civil War erupted. Unlike Texas, New Mexicans didn't side with either the North or the South. The villagers weren't pleased with the 'Bluecoats' stationed at Fort Craig, located on the Rio Grande just outside San Marcial. When General Sibley came up the Rio Grande from Texas with five thousand confederate troops and won the battle at San Marcial, Hispanics found they liked Texans even less. Sibley and his troops marched north and were eventually defeated just east of Santa Fe.

During the retreat to Texas, Sibley and his Texan troops came through Cañada Alamosa. The villagers felt sorry for them and gave them food and water. The Texans took advantage of the people, stealing some livestock and raiding some of the fields. They also insulted the people. The villagers ran them out of town hoping those filthy Texans would never come back to New Mexico, but they would come back.

After the Civil War another invasion of New Mexico occurred. Silver was discovered on the south end of the Black Range and Mogollon Mountains and miners began to setup camps. This was Apache country. The Apaches raided the mining camps and killed many miners. The United States government quickly stepped in to stop the killing of the Anglo miners and control the Apaches, relocating the tribe to a new reservation located at Ojo Caliente, a few miles north of Cañada Alamosa.

Perfecto Martinez traded with the Apaches at the new reservation and made friends with an older man there. Since Perfecto was part Apache, it was likely they accepted his friendship. The older Apache would talk with Perfecto when he came to trade.

It was now 1873. Perfecto and Lucas had six children, including Epitacio, who was the oldest son. In April 1873 Lucas gave birth to twin baby boys, named Patrocinio and Senon.

Three cultures were now in the Alamosa valley: Anglos, Indians, and Hispanics. Perfecto was looking for a new location to settle, a place with plenty of water and grass for livestock and it must have fertile ground for planting. The old Apache told him he knew a place and there were already a few Hispanics settled there.

The old Apache knew of the valley because it was part of the Apache's land before the United States government moved them to the Ojo Caliente reservation. The valley stretched west of the San Mateo Mountains and beyond the San Augustin Plains. There was a small fort there called Aragon. Perfecto pondered what the old Apache told him and decided he would move his family.

Why these settlers continued to wander is interesting. For Perfecto, was it a yearning to return to the homeland of his mother's people? Was it an innate instinct for adventure and discovery? Or was it just a continuing desire to find a better life? He went back to the reservation and asked the old Apache to guide him to the beautiful valley. The old man agreed.

The twins were several months old when Perfecto and Lucas packed the ox wagons with all eight children and as much of the household goods they could carry and departed to their new home. The old Apache led the way on his horse.

Coming north up the Rio Grande in his ox wagon, it is very likely Perfecto's family may have stopped at Jose Miguel Baca's, Elfego's grandfather's, mercantile store in Socorro to pick up supplies as it was along the their route.

It took several weeks to travel the approximately two hundred miles. It is presumed they traveled around the San Mateo Mountains and across the San Augustin Plains, and then west on an Apache trail across the Continental Divide. All the time on the journey Perfecto prayed the old Apache was not leading them to their death.

When the little caravan crossed the Continental Divide on a bald ridge of the Tularosa Mountains, the countryside and vegetation changed dramatically and they looked from the north end into the vast valley below. A clear water stream called the Tularosa flowed toward the southwest from the highlands. As it neared its junction with the San Francisco River, it softened and cut a wide path through the valley. The valley, varying from one to three miles wide, fanned into numerous meadows. Mountains lay to the south, heavily timbered with pine, which would provide timber for building and heat. Mesas rose to the northwest. Juniper and *piñon* shared the valley with pale willows and cottonwoods along the stream. The flatlands were lush with grama grass and dotted with yellow and purple flowers.

At one wide spot along the river stood the little village and Fort Aragon, about fifteen miles northeast of the present-day town of Reserve, New Mexico. Perfecto Martinez chose a location for his ranch and unloaded his family. Unlike other settlers, he did not build his house around the Aragon plaza for protection. He constructed a log cabin on a hillside above the creek, with higher hills behind it. This cabin had shuttered windows and a fireplace for cooking and heating. Perfecto tilled land in the valley for corn, beans, and wheat, and ranged cattle across the unfenced grazing area around him.

It was sometime in the summer of 1873 when Epitacio Martinez arrived with his parents and siblings to the San Francisco valley. Epitacio, now a teenager, would live his entire life in this small valley. The people of this valley, banded together for protection and companionship, would be his extended family.

More Hispanic families arrived in the area and soon additional villages sprouted along the San Francisco River. The villages were named: Upper Frisco, Middle Frisco, and Lower Frisco Plazas. Sometime after 1873 Lucas's brother, Espedion Armijo and family, built a ranch near Epitacio's family, but closer to Upper Frisco Plaza.

Life was never easy for these settlers on such a remote outpost. Some of the settlers could not survive the hardships and continuing Indian attacks and returned to the Rio Grande valley settlements. Those settlers who would not leave the beautiful valley near the San Francisco River began building a small whitewashed Catholic Church. Saint Isidore Mission Church still stands in Lower Frisco Plaza today.

Saint Isidore Mission, established 1880, Lower Frisco, New Mexico. Photograph taken by the author, 2012.

Sometime in 1880 Perfecto Martinez was killed in the hills surrounding the area. It was thought he was killed by a band of renegade Navajos. After the funeral, Lucas' brother Espedion Armijo took charge of Perfecto's family. He convinced them to move from Aragon to Upper Frisco Plaza, where he could better help them since his ranch was nearby. Lucas and the family moved and worked Uncle Espedion's ranch. The two youngest sons, the twins Patrocinio and Senon, learned from the older ones how to care for livestock and plant seed. Epitacio was about twenty-five years old when his father was killed, the twins about seven.

After his father's death Epitacio, as the eldest son, would have shouldered family responsibilities. He would have helped to raise his younger brothers, including the twins, and without access to schooling, probably provided much of their education. It would be in his nature and upbringing to be ready to provide and defend the family.

He would, no doubt, have grown into a responsible young man. Unfortunately for Epitacio, times in the San Francisco River valley were going to change as the Texans came driving their herds. He would be forced to take a stand:

> The hope of the Spanish settlers of creating their own society and living unmolested was to be rudely shaken. Patrocinio saw the first shock waves of the Anglo civilization penetrating the gentle valleys of the San Francisco. These were lonely, sunburned men, riding tough horses and smelling of sweat, saddle leather, and wood smoke.[34]

Traveling into New Mexico, many of the Texans had inbred hatred for any Hispanic from the war with Mexico over Texas, whereas, the villagers in the San Francisco valley had little experience with Anglos, let alone Texans. These Texas cowboys were a hard breed of men.

Young, lean and full of zeal, the Texas cowboys were further toughened by the trail. Some of these men had been run out of every place they had lived and now hunted for somewhere to hide. Others were loners, men with no connections to society. Texas had a surplus of such men to export to New Mexico. They were men who found it healthy to stay far beyond the reach of the Texas Rangers. They supported themselves by running the trails, killing, and rustling.

By 1884 more Texans had come to work on the ranches around the San Francisco valley and the Hispanic villagers and Anglos had a violent clash. It was autumn, the time to gather beans, bring wagonloads of wood from the forests, string peppers, and hunt deer before winter set in, but this was no ordinary fall in the valley. Trouble in the Plazas was coming to a boiling point.

The villagers came to fear the Texans. For one thing, the Texans were helping themselves to the free community grazing land, which had been a point of Spanish law as long as anyone could remember. Local calves were disappearing and the Hispanic ranchers blamed the Texans. The Martinez brothers heard the talk of the people and witnessed the behavior of the Texas cowboys. Were all Anglos such wild and coarse people as these? Would they have to live with such people, with no one to help them?

Neither race felt any inclination for sociability or understanding toward the other. Respectable Hispanic women secluded themselves in their homes with little chance for socializing, for fear of the rude Texans. Unfortunately, the Hispanic men would meet the Anglos when they went to Upper Frisco Plaza to purchase liquor and supplies.

San Francisco River valley, New Mexico. Photograph taken by the author, 2011.

The San Francisco valley provided the two main requirements for cattle: good grasslands and good water. The San Francisco River winds its way from the Apache-Sitgreaves National Forest in northern Arizona into New Mexico. It meanders south and then west again for approximately 159 miles, until it joins the Gila River in southern Arizona. Sections of the river are calm and shallow as it winds through valleys, such as in Reserve. In other areas, it is rugged and used today by kayakers and white-water enthusiasts. The San Francisco River valley would have been an obvious path for cattle drovers. Around 1883 Texans began arriving to the San Francisco River valley bringing cattle to feed on the open range. This could only mean trouble for both the Hispanic villagers and the Texas cowboys. Captain William French came to be working in the valley during this time and describes the Texan mentality:

> To explain this interesting outbreak, locally known as 'The Mexican War', it is necessary to enter slightly into history. During the years between 1883 and 1885 a number of cattlemen had moved their herds, and occasionally their neighbours' herds, from Texas to New Mexico. This migration was generally in the way of business, but sometimes its object was to avoid unpleasant consequences of not too strict observance of the law. A new brand, a new name, and a new country covered a multitude of sins. Amongst those whose absence from Texas was tolerated only on the grounds of saving expense to the State where many cowboys who lost no opportunity of displaying their hatred of Mexicans. To them all Mexicans were 'Greasers' and unfit associates for white men.[35]

Around this time a man named William Riley Milligan, one of many discharged United States soldiers, opened a liquor emporium in Upper Frisco Plaza. It was the nearest place the Texas cowboys could buy liquor and they would frequent it often.

One of the largest ranches in the area was the John B. Slaughter Ranch located near Upper Frisco Plaza. The Slaughter cowboys would ride into town to drink at Milligans. With safety in numbers, the Slaughter cowboys 'ruled the town.'

By the early 1880s, the Hispanic villagers not only had Apaches to contend with, but Texans. The Texas cowboys would come to Milligans and get liquored up on their off hours. This meant trouble for the Hispanic residents. The drunken cowboys would start shooting dogs, chickens, into houses, and anything that moved. To the Texas cowboy this was what they called 'treeing a town.' Treeing was Texas cowboys on their worst behavior — drinking, fighting, terrorizing, and shooting while riding wildly up and down the street.

Epitacio Martinez, as an older man with his daughter Encarnacion and wife Soledad. Photograph courtesy of the Martinez family.

It was in front of Milligan's Liquor Emporium where Epitacio Martinez braved his life for another Hispanic villager, *el Burro*, against the Texas cowboys while they were 'treeing the town.' *El Burro* was castrated and Epitacio was shot four times by the cowboys. Not even the law of the town could stop these wild men. No one, but Elfego Baca.

The Slaughters

By the 1870s as many as five million cattle, both wild and branded, roamed the Texas plains. Trails led from Texas through Abilene to Kansas. The Goodnight-Loving Trail looped from central Texas into New Mexico and then straight north to Cheyenne, Wyoming, for a marathon 700-mile trek:

> Men as wild and tough as the longhorns were hired to round-up and drive these ownerless Texas cattle on the "long drive," the slow, dangerous journey to the stations. During the decades following the Civil War, over 40,000 men were employed to herd cattle in the West. These "Cowboys" were usually in their twenties and came from many backgrounds. Contrary to the Hollywood film image, being a cowboy involved hard work, low pay, constant exposure to the elements, and a notable absence of many things we now consider necessities such as bathing, a change of clothes, and a diet more diverse than boiled beef and beans.
>
> The Texas cattle carried a tick-borne disease that infected the eastern cattle. The disease produced no symptoms in the longhorns, but it was devastating to the eastern breeds. Kansas ranchers of blooded stock complained to the state legislature about infected Texas cattle.

> In 1872, the legislature drew a quarantine line south of Abilene, Kansas, beyond which it was illegal to move Texas cattle. John McCoy moved his operation to Wichita, Kansas, which then had a four-year run as a roaring cattle town along with the towns of Caldwell and Ellsworth. In 1876, the quarantine line was redrawn south of Wichita, and the long-drive cattle trade moved west to Dodge City, Kansas, and north to Cheyenne, Wyoming. These rough outposts on the frontier welcomed the cattle drives and catered to the cowboys for the dollars they brought into the community. Cowboys were young men with no personal attachment to these towns, however, which often meant trouble.[36]

The tick quarantine of 1876 drove Texas cattle barons away from the Kansas trail to the trails through New Mexico to Wyoming. From Wyoming the cattle were herded into packed train cars for the long trip east to a waiting market. The trail through New Mexico brought Texas cattle through the peaceful San Francisco valley. Many cattle ranchers came into the rich Frisco valley in the 1880s including the Slaughter brothers, Will and John. Some cattle outfits were merely traveling through on the open range to Wyoming. The Slaughters setup ranching operations in the Frisco valley for a number of years on a more permanent basis.

George Webb Slaughter, father of John B. Slaughter, had been running cattle on the plains of Texas since 1857.

He was born in Mississippi in 1811. It is believed George's ancestors came from England before the Revolutionary War and were granted land in Virginia near the James River in 1620. Walter Slaughter, a descendent of the original English immigrants, fought in the Revolutionary War. After the Revolutionary War, Walter married Margaret Webb, and in 1790 Walter and his wife Margaret moved to Washington County Georgia. They lived there until they died.

George's father, William, married Nancy Anne Moore and moved to Louisiana in 1825 and bought a farm and worked it for several years. George Webb Slaughter was their first son. During his youth, George managed to attend school only a few weeks, which was the only schooling he ever had. Education seemed less important in those days than skill with pistol and rifle, which was used more frequently than pen and parchment.[37]

Many Louisianans were moving west. Land was cheap in Texas and William Slaughter had plans for his family. Unfortunately, his wife Nancy died before the final plans to move to Texas were completed. Around 1830 William Slaughter moved his family of four boys and four girls to Texas, to an area called the Sabine District. George accompanied his father to Texas and would have arrived in Texas at about nineteen years old.

The Sabine District where the William Slaughter family first settled in Texas in 1830 was not too stable a municipality, due to its proximity to the old Neutral Ground extending from Arroyo Hondo on the east to the Sabine on the west. This neutral area was established after the Louisiana Purchase when the United States and Spain could not agree on the boundary between Louisiana and Texas. As a result, settlers from either territory were not permitted to live in the strip, allowing many outlaws and other criminal types to find refuge there. In fact, in 1810 and 1812 the United States and Spanish governments sent joint military expeditions to the neutral ground to drive out outlaws who were making travel through the strip too dangerous. Americans wanting to colonize in Texas, who made it safely across this dangerous zone, arrived in the Mexican territory of Texas. Sabine County was not organized until 1837 and was commonly called the District of the Department of Nacogdoches when the Slaughter family moved there.

In 1830, the Mexican government required Anglo settlers coming to the Texas territory to be Catholic or convert to being Catholic. This was the agreement between Moses Austin when he negotiated the contract with the Spanish government to bring Anglo colonists from the United States into Texas. The agreement, however, was impossible to enforce.

The Slaughters refused or didn't become Catholic and were essentially illegal aliens in the Mexican territory of Texas. Non-Catholics were only able to acquire land by buying it from original Catholic owners, who had previously received land grants from the Spanish Crown. Many others, such as Sam Houston, were thought to have accepted Catholicism only in practice and not conviction, as a way to become a citizen and acquire land and position in Texas.

By 1840 only a small Hispanic population remained in the Sabine, most of whom had now become largely assimilated, and the town of Nacogdoches lost most of its colonial character.

As stated earlier in the Texas chapter of this book, the colonists rebelled against the Mexican government, because they perceived the Mexican government was strict and tyrannical, and they wanted the freedom they enjoyed in the continental United States. William Slaughter and his son, George, joined the colonists' fight against the Mexican government.

The strict enforcement of the Mexican laws and a forced adherence to the Catholic faith, the only religion permitted, left an indelible mark on George Slaughter and may have played a major part in his decision to become an ordained Baptist minister a decade later.

When Texas became a Republic, the Slaughters received generous land grants. William received one league and one labor of land located in Burnet County and his son, George Webb Slaughter, received one league and one labor in Smith County. One league contained 4,428 acres, and one labor contained 177 acres. The Slaughters were now rightful landowners in Texas.

John Bunyan Slaughter was born in Sabine County in 1848. He was the fourth son of George and Nancy Slaughter. It was said that John was born a cattleman. He grew up on the back of a horse, riding and roping. He learned to understand cattle at an early age. At seventeen he was given the position of cowboy and helped his father on cattle drives. He was paid $15 a month. John learned about most of the trails and campgrounds and water holes in West Texas, New Mexico, Indian territory, and Kansas.

John hired on as a cowboy for cattle drives and on one such drive with a neighbor named McAdams, an electrical storm stampeded the cattle in Montague County near Victoria Peak. The crew had to wait till morning to roundup the scattered herd. In the morning the men separated to find the herd and by nightfall had most of the herd contained, however McAdams and a young cowboy had not returned.

Three days later vultures circling in the sky attracted the attention of the cowboys, and riding forward to investigate, they found the bodies of the two missing men scalped and mutilated. The heart of one victim had been cut out and placed on his stomach.

The cattleman's life on the Texas frontier was a hard life which John embraced. He was a hard man who lived through hard times, fought Indians in hand-to-hand combat, was shot through the chest, rode the wilds of the west driving cattle, and was well respected for his cattle knowledge:

> **In adult years, though a man of small stature, John rated big in the pioneer cattle industry of Texas.**[38]

Later in the 1870s John and his younger brother Will created a partnership, deciding to push farther west into the frontier of Texas, where land was available for large herds. They staked out a ranch in Crosby County, Texas. For the next three years, John and Will continued ranching cattle and horses from this west Texas location. Life was hard on the Texas plains. Roving Indian raids and rustlers were a constant reminder this was still a wild land and life was hard for the pioneers. John's first wife, May, died in childbirth.

The 1870s tick quarantine forced the west Texas cattlemen to trail their cattle over the Goodnight-Loving Trail through New Mexico to Wyoming.

The trail into the New Mexico Territory was treacherous and the cattle had to cross deserts and mountains before the new range was reached. The Slaughter herds were among some of the first cattle to be driven from Texas into New Mexico.

Then around 1883 the State of Texas began enforcing payment, or a tax, from cattle ranchers for pasturage rights on state land. The Slaughter brothers lost or sold their Crosby County ranch to another rancher, the Spur brand of the Espuela Cattle Company. Will and John decided to move the grazing herds so they did not have to pay the state's grazing fees. It was this decision which later brought John Slaughter and his cowboys to Upper Frisco Plaza and their fateful meeting with Elfego Baca.

John and Will moved their cattle operations west into the New Mexico Territory where there was plenty of open range, and in 1883 they drove the herd to open ranges one hundred and twenty miles west of Socorro. Will made his headquarters at the American Valley [Horse Springs, NM] about thirty-nine miles northeast of Frisco Plaza and John established his headquarters along the Tularosa River somewhere northeast of Upper Frisco Plaza.

The Tularosa River flows south and into the San Francisco River near Reserve, New Mexico. In some places the river is eight to ten feet wide and in other places shallower. Typical of western rivers, spring runoff would increase the river's flow and spring rains would rejuvenate the native grasses.

Remains of corrals along the Tularosa River, northeast of Upper Frisco (modern day Reserve), New Mexico. Photograph taken by the author and Henry Martinez, 2012.

Remnants of a large cattle ranch on the Tularosa River, believed to be the Slaughter Cattle Ranch, remain today just north of Reserve. Fences, gates, and abandoned structures are built with hand-hewed logs in keeping with building methods of the 1880s.

Baca New Mexico Origins

Elfego Baca descends from a long line of hearty survivors creating his destiny to both survive and flourish. In the face of harsh surroundings, turmoil, disease and many other obstacles, Elfego's family can be traced back to the time of the *conquistadores* and the early Spanish settlements of New Mexico. The Baca's used their grit and faith to survive and Elfego followed in their footsteps.

It is possible that Elfego's ancestry stems from a Spanish war hero, Cabeza de Vaca, although this is not able to be confirmed. From the book by Fray Angélico Chávez, *Origins of New Mexico Families, A Genealogy of the Spanish Colonial Period Vol I*, and more modern tools, such as Ancestry's website, Elfego's lineage can be traced to the earliest beginnings of New Spain.

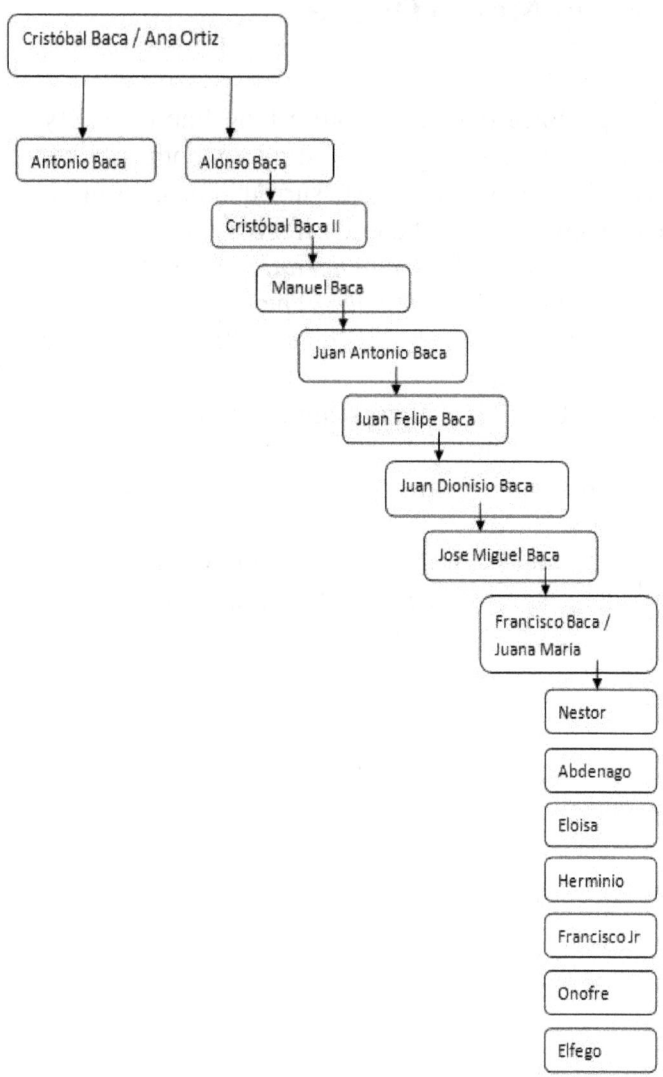

Ancestral lineage chart for Elfego Baca. Created from Author's research.

Juan de Vaca
[Born: before 1522, Mexico City, Mexico. Died: ?]

Juan de Vaca's father came to New Spain in the early 1500s with a wave of colonists from Spain and assumedly settled in or around Mexico City. Several Vacas came shortly after Cortés' discovery and conquest of the Aztec empire. Among those were Diego de Vaca, a native of Mancilla in León, and Luis Vaca, a native of Toledo. Either of these could have been the father or grandfather of Juan de Vaca. Juan, a *Criollo*, was born and lived in Mexico City. As a young man he joined Coronado's expedition into New Mexico and the northern frontier in 1540. It is assumed he was a military man chosen to accompany Coronado, since Coronado's intent was to conquer and plunder the 'seven cities of gold.' Juan de Vaca survived the two year adventure returning to Mexico City to live out his days.

One of his sons, Cristóbal, would move the Baca family to New Mexico. This move cemented the Baca family as one of the founding New Mexican families as described by Fray Angélico.

Captain Cristóbal Vaca [Baca], son of Juan de Vaca
[Born: about 1567, Mexico City, Mexico. Died: about 1613, Santa Cruz, New Mexico]

The Elfego Baca family ancestry in New Mexico dates back to Captain Cristóbal Baca, who came to reinforce Don Juan de Oñate's colony in northern New Mexico. Around 1599 Governor Oñate decided to move his headquarters and capital across the river facing the Yungue Oweenge Pueblo. The pueblo was renamed San Gabriel de los Españoles and became the capital of the Kingdom of New Mexico, as it was then known. Since the

Spaniards arrival, both the natives of the local pueblos and the Spaniards were feeling the effects of a shortage of food.

In the procurator general's list of reinforcements, Cristóbal Baca, legitimate son of Juan de Vaca, native of the city of Mexico, was listed as a man of good stature and features: swarthy, thirty-three years old, armed with coat of mail, cuisse, iron beaver, a *jineta* saddle, and his horse protected by hides of bull, cow, or calf.

Captain Cristóbal Baca and his wife Doña Ana Ortiz brought three grown daughters and one young boy to the new colony of New Mexico.

Fray Angélico Chávez in his compilation of *Origins of New Mexico Families* lists Captain Cristóbal Baca's children, who immigrated to New Mexico as: Juana de Zamora, Isabel de Bohórquez, María de Villanueva, and a boy, Antonio, all of them born in Mexico City. With them came a female servant, Ana Verdugo.[39]

Author's Note: The son listed as Antonio in Chávez' records, is now presumed to be Alonso and not Antonio. Alonso was born in Mexico City about 1589, whereas, Antonio was born about 1600. This author believes Antonio was born in New Mexico shortly after the family arrived in San Gabriel. Alonso would have been about eleven or twelve when the family moved to New Mexico, having been born in Mexico City.

It was sometime in 1600 when Captain Cristóbal Baca and family arrived to join the Oñate colony. The Baca's arrived with the reinforcements and much needed supplies for the colonists at San Gabriel. Presumably Captain Baca and his family were given housing in the new settlement. The settlement was being remodeled into a U-shaped village plan and the buildings were being changed to accommodate the life style of the Spaniards. Dome-shaped adobe ovens, much like the ones used in

Spain, were built outside. A Catholic mission, with a cruciform floor plan, was built at the opening of the U-shaped village facing the plaza.

While the remodeling was on going, Governor Oñate encouraged his priests to continue the conversion of Indians and his soldiers to search for mines. This was most important to the Spanish Crown.

There is no record of what duties were assigned to Captain Cristóbal Baca. Since he was a soldier, one would assume he would be out protecting the mining prospectors or protecting his family and the village.

In 1601 there was a mass desertion of San Gabriel by the colonists, mainly led by the Franciscan friars, leaving only about twenty-five Spanish residents:

> **The reason for their hasty departure during Oñate's absence was not hard to fathom. Many of the settlers had become bitterly disillusioned at the barren, inhospitable terrain of their new home and the meager prospects for prosperity which it offered.[40]**

Cristóbal Baca's family was among the few who remained at San Gabriel when the rest of the colonists deserted. Cristóbal was highly critical of the Franciscans and blamed them for the revolt.

Life in the New Mexico settlement was reduced to a simple formula: fending off hunger, cold, and Indians. This was not quite what the colonists had expected when they sold off their investments in New Spain, put their hopes in the new territory, and rode forth behind Oñate's standard:

> **The more affluent had packed clothing of velvet and Chinese taffeta, Cordovan**

slippers, and other finery into stout hide trunks for the trip north, expecting to use it when the silver-rich capital of their new kingdom rose in splendor on the banks of the Rio Grande. But now, less than three years later, both the garments and dreams were in tatters, and the bulk of the settlers miserably disillusioned.[41]

Most intolerable were the food shortages. The settlers struggled to plant and harvest wheat and other European crops in the rocky soil. They continued to rely upon the local Indian tribes for corn and beans, even though the Indians were more wary of sharing their meager crops. As the winter of 1601 arrived both Indian and Spanish populations bordered on starvation:

Severe winter temperatures furnished the second source of misery. Many of the Spaniards came from zones blessed with a Mediterranean or semitropical climate and thus lacked familiarity with harsh cold. Even Don Juan and his relatives who had been raised in the high, frigid uplands of Zacatecas found the bitter winters difficult to bear. "The cold is so intense," lamented a soldier, "that the rivers freeze over, and it snows most of the time during the winter, which lasts eight long months." The settlers shivered in the tiny vault-like rooms of San Gabriel, wrapped in the light blankets taken from the Indians and huddled over feeble fires whose wood had to be brought at great labor from a distance of five or six leagues. Overnight, drinking water froze in the tinajas, or pottery jars, and the sacramental wine became so cold the priests had to warm it before sunrise Mass. "May God grant us patience to bear all these hardships," wrote one man in a letter to Mexico City.[42]

Despite the hardships, the Baca family stayed loyal to Governor Oñate and remained in San Gabriel. As part of his service, Captain Cristóbal Baca commanded an escort which brought four new Franciscans from Mexico City to San Gabriel. With Cristóbal's continued residency in New Mexico and support of Oñate's governorship, he would have received the title of Don. Oñate assigned Don Cristóbal Baca as the acting Syndic, or advocate, for the Franciscan friars in 1613, however, he died sometime later that year.

His descendants survived the northern frontier and were a large part of New Mexico's history. The Baca family, Elfego's ancestors, were living in New Mexico 176 years before the Declaration of Independence was signed in Philadelphia for the fledgling United States.

Antonio Ortiz Baca, youngest son of Captain (Don) Cristóbal Baca
[Born: about 1600, San Gabriel, New Mexico. Died: 1643, Santa Fe, New Mexico]

Antonio Baca, son of Cristóbal and Ana Ortiz, lived in Santa Fe and is presumed to have been born in New Mexico after his parents arrived from Mexico City. At twenty-eight years old he was listed as a captain in the military in 1628. He married Yumar Perez de Bustillo and they had at least three daughters.

Nicolás Ortiz, a cousin of the Baca family, was a teenager and a member of an armed escort which came to Santa Fe in 1634. Young Nicolás liked Santa Fe and had family there, so he stayed, met, and married María de Bustillo.

Later in the 1630s the affairs between the civil authorities, led by Governor Luis Rosas and the church, were in turmoil. Three Franciscan priests were sent to meet with Governor Rosas in hopes of reconciling the issues. The governor attacked the friars and arrested them, although they were later released. The friars closed the church and the governor had the church demolished, using the materials for other buildings.

These actions obviously caused extreme friction between the devout Catholics and the government and troubled the Spanish crown. Around 1640 the viceroy of New Spain had Governor Rosas arrested and appointed a new governor of New Mexico. Ex-governor Rosas was detained under house arrest, until such time he could be returned to Mexico City for trial.

Nicolás Ortiz, a military man assigned to escort duty, left Santa Fe for some time leaving his young wife. When the new governor was appointed, Nicolás was assigned as an escort and returned to Santa Fe in 1641. Upon his return Nicolás found his wife, María, pregnant and living in ex-governor Rosas' home. The governor had taken María as his mistress when Nicolás was gone from Santa Fe. Nicolás was infuriated.

The Franciscans and his cousin Antonio Baca convinced Nicolás to kill ex-governor Rosas. At that time Antonio Baca was the leader of the anti-Rosas rebels and closely associated with the Franciscan friars. On the night of January 25, 1642, several masked men, including Nicolás and the Baca brothers, Alonso and Antonio, burst into ex-governor Rosas' home and killed Rosas with a sword.

Although Nicolás Ortiz, Antonio Baca, and their anti-Rosas group aligned themselves with the newly arrived governor, Pacheco, they were arrested for their actions.

Nicolás was tried and found not guilty, however, on an escort duty to New Spain he was retried, found guilty, and sentenced to hang. Nicolás Ortiz escaped and was never heard of again.

Antonio Baca, his brother Alonso, his brother-in-law Juan de Archuleta, and several friars barricaded themselves at the Santo Domingo Pueblo before they were arrested. Antonio and several others were found guilty and beheaded in 1643. Antonio Baca's head was nailed to the gibbet.

Alonso Baca was found not guilty and released. Why the brothers, Antonio and Alonso, received such different sentences for this crime is unknown, but the result for Elfego was monumental. Alonso lived and some two hundred and twenty years later Elfego Baca was born!

Alonso Ortiz Baca, son of Captain (Don) Cristóbal Baca [Born: about 1589, Mexico City, Mexico. Died: about 1662, Rio Abajo, New Mexico]

Alonso Baca is believed to be the older brother of Antonio and the direct ancestor of Elfego Baca. Fray Angélico Chávez in his writing of the *Origins of New Mexico Families* wrote information about Alonso which is confusing:

> Alonso Baca, a contemporary of Antonio, was to all appearances Antonio's younger brother [Alonso was Antonio's older brother by about ten years]. As a young captain he led a small exploratory expedition three hundred leagues into the eastern plains in 1634. He gave his age as fifty-five in 1644, but must have been a year or two younger. In the middle of the century, he uncovered a serious Indian plot. He was one of fourteen conspirators ordered executed by Governor Pacheco in 1643 (when Antonio died), but escaped death. Alonso was still living at his home in the Río Abajo district as late as 1662. Nothing more is known about him, not even his wife's name. Cristóbal Baca [II], mentioned in 1663 as *sobrino carnal* of Antonio Baca [Cristóbal was Alonso Baca's son, Antonio Baca's nephew], was apparently his son.[43]

If Alonso was Antonio's younger brother, he could not have been fifty-five in 1644. Information as to his birth in 1589 concurs with an age of fifty-five in 1643, whereas Antonio was beheaded at the age of forty-three in 1643. Perhaps Fray Chávez was referring to Alonso's looks, rather than his age, although Fray Chávez confused Antonio and Alonso earlier in the text when he wrote that Antonio was the son brought from Mexico City in 1600. Alonso was the older brother of Antonio by about ten years. Information in other internet sources supports this theory, which lists Alonso birth in 1589 in Mexico City.

Mistakes and confusion in these old records was common, such as confusing Antonio and Alonso. It can also be difficult to follow family ancestral charts due to undocumented births, deaths, marriages and the intermarriage of families. What is clear is Alonso Baca lived and had four sons and was the direct ancestor of Elfego Baca.

Cristóbal Baca II, son of Alonso Baca
[Born: about 1635, Santa Fe, New Mexico. Died: after 1687?]

Cristóbal Baca is referred to as a nephew of Antonio and son of Alonso. He signed the muster-roll, a military roster, as a captain and was married with three sons and three daughters. He was son-in-law of Diego de Trujillo, both of whom were persecuted by the ill-famed Governor López Mendizábal (1659 – 1661). In the footsteps of ex-governor Rosas, Governor López fought with the Franciscan friars and was later removed from office and returned to Mexico City by the Spanish Inquisition.[44] Cristóbal, like his father and uncle, Antonio, stood with the Franciscans and the Catholic Church against the government.

His wife was Ana Moreno de Lara and though his exact death is unknown, Cristóbal must have been dead by 1687, when only she and some of their children are mentioned. The family would have been living in New Mexico during the Pueblo Revolt beginning in 1680 and fled to El Paso. This explains why the family was not in Santa Fe and Cristóbal died while the family was in exile in El Paso. The daughters, Catalina, Juana and Luisa, and the sons, José, Manuel, and Ignacio, are mentioned with their father Cristóbal in the Muster-roll of 1682.[45]

Manuel Baca, son of Cristóbal Baca II
[Born: about 1656, Santa Fe, New Mexico. Died: before 1727, Bernalillo, New Mexico]

Manual Baca, surviving brother of Ignacio and José, fled with the family during the Pueblo Revolt. He returned to New Mexico in 1693 with his wife María de Salazar and a growing family. Soon after, he re-established himself at Bernalillo on lands which belonged to his father, Cristóbal Baca II. In 1716 he gathered forty Queres Indians for the Moqui Campaign and also led the Albuquerque contingent. The Indians of the three Queres Pueblos of Cochití, Santo Domingo, and San Felipe complained more than once of mistreatment by him and his sons and for this cause he was deprived of the *Alcaldía* of Cochití in 1718 and sentenced to go on the next two forays against infidel Indians. Both he and his wife were dead by 1727.

The Bacas, Archuletas, Chávez, Luceros, and Montoyas were some of the original New Mexico settlers who returned to New Mexico with Don Diego de Vargas. These families lived in exile at Guadalupe del Paso (current day El Paso, Texas) for thirteen years during the Pueblo Revolt of 1680 to 1693. While there the families grew, probably some members of their families stayed at Guadalupe del Paso, with others returning to New Mexico after the rebellion. It would become evident later in Elfego's life that some of the extended Baca family stayed and flourished in the El Paso area, while others, such as Manuel and family, Elfego's direct ancestors, returned to New Mexico.

Juan Antonio Baca, son of Manuel Baca
[Born: about 1696, Bernalillo, New Mexico. Died: before 1762, Santa Fe, New Mexico]

Juan Antonio Baca, son of Manuel, was born after the reconquest of New Mexico. He and his first wife, María Gallegos, had one daughter, Teodora. It is presumed María died and he then married Petronila García Jurado, by whom he had five children: Rafaela, Juan Francisco, Juan Miguel, Juan Felipe, and Miguel Antonio. Juan and his family returned to the Santa Fe area where he later died.

Juan Felipe Baca, son of Juan Antonio Baca
[Born: about 1740, Santa Fe, New Mexico. Died: ?, Belen, New Mexico]

Little information is known about Juan Felipe Baca, except that he and his family relocated from Santa Fe to Belen, New Mexico.

Juan Dionisio Baca, son of Juan Felipe Baca
[Born: about 1765, Belen, New Mexico. Died: after 1845, Socorro, New Mexico]

Don Juan Dionisio Baca was documented to have lived in several locations near the Belen and Socorro areas, as so noted by birth locations of his ten children. One interesting note is his designation of *Don*.[46] Don Juan Baca was a land owner and *hidalgo* in the Socorro area. The Baca family had earned the status of *hidalgo* through Captain (Don) Cristóbal Baca's service to Governor Oñate.

Jose Miguel Baca, son of Juan Dionisio Baca, grandfather of Elfego Baca
[Born: about 1799, Los Bacas, New Mexico. Died: 1872, Socorro New Mexico]

Jose Miguel Baca was born in 1799 in Los Bacas, New Mexico, a location which is believed to be the lands of Don Juan Dionisio. He married María Dolores Velarde and established a merchandizing store in San Marcial, New Mexico, just south of Socorro. San Marcial was an old stop-over on *el Camino Real*, or the King's Highway, supporting travelers between Mexico City and Santa Fe. Jose later relocated his merchandizing business to Socorro where he and María raised their children.

It was Elfego's grandfather who established the Baca family into the merchandizing business in New Mexico. Elfego Baca would work in the family's store in Socorro as a young man. While he was working in the mercantile, Pedro Sarracino came to Socorro reporting the trouble in the San Francisco valley with the Texas cowboys and seeking help. Elfego answered the call.

Francisco Baca, son of Jose Miguel Baca, father of Elfego Baca
[Born: 1834, San Marcial, New Mexico. Died: ?]

Francisco Baca, father of Elfego Baca, was born in 1834 at San Marcial, New Mexico, before his father Jose moved the family business to Socorro. Francisco married Juana María Baca on December 17, 1855, in Socorro, New Mexico.

From all accounts Francisco pursued his father's merchandizing business, and he acquired substantial property. He was a also respected land owner and cattle rancher in Socorro County.

The 1860 census lists Francisco as merchant and farmer, with $600 in personal and $3,500 in real property, a considerable amount of wealth for that day.[47]

Elfego Baca was the youngest son of Francisco and Juana Baca. He was born in Socorro, New Mexico. His baptismal record shows he was baptized on February 15, 1865, when he was five days old. He was the youngest of seven children; the oldest was Nestor. He had other siblings: Abdenago, Eloisa, Herminio, Francisco Jr., and Onofre. Nestor was the oldest and Elfego the youngest, however, exact sibling order of the other children is not certifiable. Where and when Elfego's father Francisco died is also not known.

Young Elfego

Sometime in the year 1866 Francisco Baca moved his family from Socorro, New Mexico, to Topeka, Kansas, when Elfego was an infant of no more than a year old. Elfego later stated in his autobiography that his father took the family to Kansas to give them a better education than they would get in Socorro. If the 1860 census is correct, Francisco had the financial resources to make this move. It is not totally clear why Francisco felt the need to uproot his family. Perhaps, it was an innate Spanish need for adventure and discovery or he was lured by financial prospects.

Kansas became a state in 1861, only five years before Francisco Baca and family arrived in Topeka. The Kansas capital began to grow and prosper after the Civil War. The Atchison, Topeka and Santa Fe Railway Company was headquartered in Topeka. The company was chartered to build a rail line from Topeka, Kansas to Santa Fe, New Mexico, and then on to the Gulf of Mexico. During this time period Topeka offered many opportunities for anyone willing to work. Francisco started his own business as a 'minor contractor' in Topeka, a business he kept for the fifteen years the family lived in Topeka. It is not known what type of contracting business he conducted or whether it involved the railroad.

Author's Note: Several biographies have been written about Elfego Baca. He wrote his autobiography titled, *Here Comes Elfego!*, from which he used excerpts for political pamphlets later in life. Elfego teamed up with Kyle S. Crichton to write his life story in 1928. In that autobiography, Elfego dictated his version of his life to Crichton. The Crichton book, *Law And Order, Ltd.*, remains as the main source for researchers looking for information on Elfego's life up to 1928. These stories of Elfego's life contain discrepancies that cannot be resolved. In the following chapter some of these anomalies will be pointed out. The truth will remain a mystery.

In February of 1865 Elfego's mother, Juanita, was playing a game called *Las Iglesias*, a game similar to the game we now call softball. She was nine months pregnant with Elfego. Elfego called her short and stubby, so that when a ball came her way she jumped to catch the ball and 'here comes Elfego.' Needless to say, the game was stopped and mother and newborn were taken into the house and cared for. 'Here Comes Elfego' became a fitting axiom for the man who would become the famous Elfego Baca.

Elfego was an infant when his father and mother left Socorro in the spirit of their Spanish ancestors and explorers before them. The family set out on an expedition packing up their belongings and joining an ox caravan heading to Topeka, Kansas, and like their ancestors before them, the Baca family encountered Indian trouble.

Ox caravan in the streets of Socorro. Photograph reproduction courtesy of the Socorro Historical Society.

Interestingly, Elfego's brother Onofre did not travel with the family to Kansas, staying instead in Socorro with relatives. He was listed on the 1880 census of Socorro as living with Gregorio and Maria Demetria Baca. Their son, Abrán, was listed as 19 and Onofre as 17. Onofre was listed as 'son,' but it is evident the word 'son' was overwritten on what appears to be the word 'ward.'

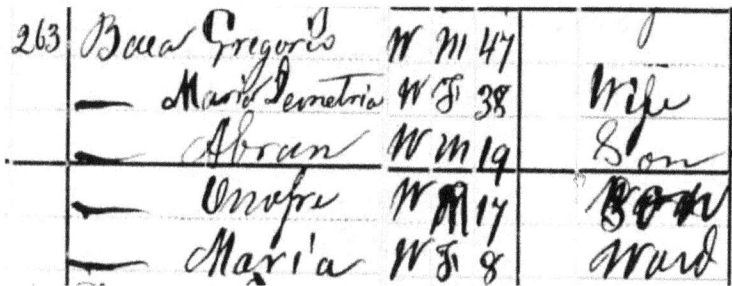

Excerpt of 1880 Census information for Onofre Baca.

However, it should be noted, the 1870 census lists Abrán as 12 years old and does not list Onofre, raising the possibility that Onofre went to Kansas and then returned to live with his aunt and uncle in New Mexico at some point. The 1880 census, ten years later, lists Abrán as 19 and Onofre as 17. Why the discrepancy on Abrán's age on these two census reports is unknown. It is believed Onofre started living in Socorro with Gregorio in 1866 when he did not accompany the family to Kansas. Onofre would have been approximately five or six years old when the family left for Topeka.

The aunt and uncle only had one son, Abrán, and no daughters. It may not have been unusual in the day to leave young Onofre with his aunt and uncle and young cousin. It is also obvious from the census record they cared for a young girl, Maria, as a ward. Also interesting they overwrote the word 'son' for Onofre, but left Maria as 'ward.' Why Onofre did not go with the family is unknown, but will later dramatically affect his life and death.

Presumably without Elfego's brother, Onofre, the Baca family left Socorro and headed to Topeka. When the ox caravan neared Estancia, now the county seat of Torrance County, New Mexico, the caravan was attacked by Navajos on the warpath and they kidnapped the infant Elfego. After several days they brought him back and tossed him to his mother. In those days the Navajos were known to boil infants in hot oil or grab them by the heels and slam their heads against a rock. The story of the incident is quite colorful:

> Master Baca was returned to his parents at the end of two days none the worse for his experience. This constitutes, according to Mr. Baca and his friends, the first incident in a long and agitated career which entitled him to the subsequent tag of "charmed." Detractors of Mr. Baca contend just as forcibly — but outside the presence and earshot of Mr. Baca — that the infant Elfego was boiled in oil for two days with nothing resulting but a lovely pink hue denoting the best of health and that he rebounded at such pace when swung against the rock as to quite upset — literally and figuratively — the good chieftain who had undertaken the pleasurable deed.[48]

No one knows for certain what happened to the infant Elfego when and if the Navajos took him to their campground. But it is a fact; they did bring him back to his mother. Like his ancestors before him, perhaps the Spanish War Saint Santiago and a band of angels saved Elfego from certain death or perhaps he was destined to survive.

It is not known exactly where Francisco Baca settled his family in Topeka. Larry D. Ball in his biography of Elfego surmised they lived in the Oakland community, which later became a Hispanic Barrio. However, Elfego recollected that his Spanish was only picked up from the household and he was not fluent. No census information has been located for the family in the 1870 Kansas census.

While the Baca family lived in Topeka, Elfego's sister Eloisa died on February 18, 1872, and his mother died on March 1, 1872. Seven days later his brother Herminio died. No documents have survived as to what caused their deaths, although one could assume some contagious disease such as influenza or cholera. Both were prevalent at the time and may have been the cause. Elfego, his father Francisco and brothers Nestor, Abdenago, and Francisco Jr. survived the epidemic.

In his autobiographies, Elfego stated after his mother died he was sent back to Socorro to live with his grandparents, without identifying his age. Elfego would have been seven years old when his mother and siblings died. Larry D. Ball, Howard Bryan and Stan Sager wrote Elfego was put in an orphanage until the age of fifteen, then he returned to Socorro. They stated the reference for the orphanage story from Abe B. Baca, a nephew of Elfego, from an interview he gave in 1981.[49]

Elfego said his oldest brother, E. B. Baca (presumably Nestor), became stray and went traveling in all directions. He was never heard of again. Elfego's biographers state his father, Francisco, and brother, Abdenago, left Elfego in a Topeka orphanage and went to Colorado to seek employment and presumably search for

Nestor. They surmised it would account for the 'lost' years between 1872 and 1880, at which time Elfego and his brother Abdenago returned to Socorro.

However, it is hard to believe Elfego's father would put his youngest child in an orphanage and leave the state to seek employment in another state. The prospects for work in Topeka at the time were good, since the Atchison, Topeka and Santa Fe Railway project was fully under way. There must have been plenty of work in Topeka. It is more likely his father would have left him to live with friends or family, before consigning him to an orphanage.

From this author's interview with Elfego's grandnephew Gil Baca, he refutes the story of Abe B. Baca and the orphanage. He does not believe Elfego spent any time in an orphanage in Topeka. Gil remembers stories told at family gatherings by his mother, aunts, and uncles. They said Elfego's father was a well-off man and would never put Elfego in an orphanage. Furthermore, Elfego never mentioned being placed in an orphanage in his autobiography written by Kyle S. Crichton.

Elfego's older brother, Abdenago, would have been twelve or thirteen when their mother died, while Nestor would have been about sixteen at that time. Their last remaining sibling, Francisco Jr., would have been about one year older than Elfego. It seems unlikely Elfego's father left the three children for any length of time and even more unlikely that he put any of them in an orphanage. It should be noted here, references to Elfego's brother Francisco Jr. are absent. The whereabouts or death of both Nestor and Francisco Jr. are unknown, but it is known Elfego, Abdenago, and their father Francisco returned to Socorro in 1880.

There are some more details to support the theory that Elfego was not placed in an orphanage. Elfego was a friend of Charles Curtis, a school mate, while attending school in Topeka. Charles Curtis went on to become the vice-president of the United States under the presidency of Herbert Hoover. Elfego's friendship with Charles Curtis is well documented, forcing us to believe he attended school in Topeka and did not return to Socorro until later in life, and was not living in an orphanage.

Charles Curtis's life is documented in *From Kaw Teepee To Capitol, The Life of Charles Curtis, Indian, Who Has Risen to High Estate* by Don C. Seitz. Charles Curtis was born on January 25, 1860, making him about five years older than Elfego. His father, Orren Arms Curtis, was a Captain in the Cavalry nicknamed 'Captain Jack.' His mother was Ellen Pappan Curtis and was part Kansa/Kaw Indian. She died in April of 1863, when Charles was three, of 'black fever' as cholera was called in those days. It was the custom of the Kaw for Charles to live with his maternal grandparents on the Kaw reservation. By 1873 his maternal grandmother believed Charles would amount to nothing on the reservation and advised him to go and live with his paternal grandparents in Eugene located in north Topeka.

Charles' father, Orren, constructed a saloon in Eugene around 1858. The saloon was the place where Topeka celebrated when the first train arrived on January 1, 1866. Subsequently, Orren started construction on the Curtis House Hotel, a livery stable, a general store, a post office, a feed lot, and a warehouse for the exclusive use of the railroad. Charles lived in the hotel with his grandparents.

Charles' grandfather, William Curtis, built a race track in Eugene for training horses and for the entertainment of the locals. People from both sides of the Kansas River came to the race-track to win or lose money. Charles knew about horses from his youth on the reservation where horse racing was very popular. Horse racing on the Kaw reservation usually involved betting against the best horses of the Potawatomis, Osages, and white settlers at county fairs in eastern Kansas.

Charles became one of the best riders in Eugene, now know as North Topeka, from the late 1860s to 1876 when he became a full-fledged jockey racing all over the state. Charles finished elementary school in 1875 and continued racing horses until 1876, before he entered Topeka High School. Later in life, Charles Curtis went on to serve six terms in the House of Representatives and six terms as a United States Senator, before becoming the thirty-first Vice President of the United States under President Herbert Hoover in 1929.

Charles Curtis as a young man of approximately eighteen years old.

This brief narrative above on Charles Curtis may have some clues about the Baca family life in Topeka. Elfego mentioned only a few recollections about his stay in Topeka. One was he only knew one other Hispanic family, named Sanchez. Another was about his friendship with a school mate named Charles Curtis. How their lives intertwined is not completely understood, except this friendship could only have happened if Elfego was living in Kansas, and it would be doubtful if Elfego was in an orphanage.

Although Charles Curtis was about five years older, he started his formal education late since he was raised on the Kaw reservation. He came to Topeka and started elementary school as an older boy. Could this be when Elfego and he met and became friends? Charles was part-Indian; Elfego was Hispanic. Did they live and go to school in the same area of Topeka?

Francisco Baca may have been a 'minor contractor' for Orren Curtis on his various construction projects in Topeka. Francisco may also have done work for railroad projects. Perhaps Francisco learned about racehorses at the Curtis racetrack and it may explain why he bought a racing quarter horse when he returned to Socorro.

In his autobiography *Here Comes Elfego!*, Elfego said after his mother died he went to live with his grandparents in Socorro. He did not elaborate on his years in Topeka. He did mention that he was fifteen when he and his brother Abdenago returned to Socorro, which was in 1880. Elfego indicated his father, Francisco, stayed in Topeka to close up his affairs; which affairs are unknown or perhaps he was finishing some contracting. Based on documented events, his father had returned to Socorro by late 1880.

It was written that Francisco and Juana left Socorro for Topeka in 1865 or 1866 for the educational advantages for the family and probably for work. Socorro was a small village. In 1833 the Socorro census listed about 400 residents in the village with about 1,774 in the Socorro area. The population was predominantly Spanish-speaking and of Hispanic decent. Elfego was approximately seven when his mother died. By all accounts he was proficient in English and was an educated young man when he returned to Socorro in 1880. Elfego must have grown up speaking some Spanish in the home. However, he would have grown proficient in English, if he stayed in elementary school and gone on to high school in Topeka. Later in life he went on to study law. It has to be assumed he finished a higher amount of schooling in Topeka. When he returned to Socorro, a primarily Spanish-speaking community, Elfego said he was not proficient in Spanish and could only talk a little in Spanish. It is obvious that his education in Topeka was at English-speaking schools.

Orphanages in the 1870s were not happy places. It is doubtful that Elfego would have become as educated, if he spent his formative years in an orphanage. However, it may be likely he and Francisco Jr. were supported by friends in the community while his father was working or searching for Nestor from time to time, or because his mother was dead — perhaps even with Charles Curtis' family.

Elfego Baca at the age of fifteen, shortly after his return to Socorro, New Mexico. Photograph reproduction courtesy of the private collection of Gilbert Baca, Elfego Baca's grandnephew, Rio Rancho, New Mexico.

For the time period of this picture, Elfego was certainly dressed as a young gentleman. He looks every bit the part of an educated young man of the time, whether in Topeka or Socorro.

In his autobiography, Elfego said when he was sixteen he went to work at his grandparent's cattle ranch as a cowboy somewhere near Socorro. According to other timelines of stories, it is more likely that he was still fifteen.

Elfego detailed accounts of meeting and hanging out with Billy the Kid in Albuquerque in late 1880 or early 1881. This is his account of that time of his life:

> At that time I must have been about 16 years old when I met Billy the Kid at a round-up at a certain place [about 12 miles] northeast of Socorro called [Ojo de] "La Parida Ranch".[50]

He said there were over forty cowboys there, rounding up and branding cattle. It was at the roundup he met Billy the Kid. He said Billy was fluent in Spanish and he, Elfego, was not good at speaking Spanish.

He and Billy rode their horses from La Parida Ranch to the Isleta Pueblo, left their horses there, and then hopped a rail cart to Albuquerque. Elfego wrote about the adventure with Billy when they got to Albuquerque:

> That night Billy and I camped under a big cotton[wood] tree, the site being where the Sturges Hotel is now, [101 First St. SW, now a vacant lot] at that time it was a saloon. Billy and I were wondering what we were going to do when here comes a policeman and shot a man about five or six times. The policeman went into the saloon and called the boys to have a drink. About that time here comes [Sheriff] Perfecto Armijo and said, "Who killed that man out there?" The policeman said, "I did, what about it?" Perfecto then caught him with the left hand by the shirt collar and with the right hand from the rear end of his body and picked him up just like a cat will pick up a mouse.

This policeman was tried and convicted to be hung and was hung.[51]

Below Elfego continues his adventures with the roguish Billy the Kid:

> Then Billy and I went to Old Town which was wide open, liquor of all kinds, women of all kinds. Billy carried a little pistol called a Bulldog Repeater, when if fired it made a strong noise perhaps louder than a .45 gun. We went into a Saloon called Martinez Saloon where there was dancing, gambling, and every other thing. Billy and I went out. Billy thought the town was more silent than what he expected it. He then fired a shot up in the air and it made an awful strong noise.
> Here comes the Deputy Sheriff, a very brave man by the name by Cornelio Murphy. He searched both of us and he was very mad. Billy made most of the talking to him in Spanish. The Deputy charged us of having fired that shot but he couldn't find the pistol. The Deputy walked away, so did we.
> The deputy must have been about one block away when Billy fired two more shots. The deputy came back as mad as a man could be and searched us again, he called us every name that he could think of. Anyhow we went back to the Martinez Saloon. While in the Saloon,

> Billy fired one more shot and the lights went out.
>
> Billy and I determined to leave the place and we did. Every time Billy fired a shot he put it under his hat, it was a stiff, Derby hat. Then Billy and I continued to stay around Albuquerque and vicinity perhaps a couple of weeks.[52]

He goes on to say he took on a job in south Albuquerque in a neighborhood area called Barelas. In Barelas he worked for a man named Francisco Apodaca. He and Francisco's son, Pedro, hauled ham for the roundhouse of the Atchison, Topeka and Santa Fe Railway Company. Sometime after the job in Barelas, Elfego returned to Socorro.

Billy the Kid historians have disputed Elfego's story based on other accounts of Billy's whereabouts, but Elfego has clearly stated this story in both his autobiographies.

Trouble in Socorro

In the 1880s with the new railroad stop at Socorro, the Hispanic inhabitants saw an influx of Anglo miners, merchants, and cattlemen. Mines and smelters added a greater importance to the town of Socorro. Texas cattlemen began developing cattle ranges in the western precincts of the county. With the cattlemen came Texas cowboys and their 'Remember the Alamo' attitude. Socorro was growing and animosity between Anglo and Hispanic Americans was also growing.

Train Station, Socorro, New Mexico, circa 1880s. Photograph reproduction courtesy of the Socorro Historical Society.

Elfego made the following statement to his biographer, Crichton, about the animosity between the Anglos and the Hispanics in Socorro when he returned as a young man:

> "As a matter of fact I was afraid of what they called Mexicans."[53]

It is interesting that Elfego hardly discussed stories from his Topeka youth. Perhaps life was much quieter in Topeka than Socorro or perhaps he was now a teenager, almost a man, engaging in life on the western frontier. In Topeka, his friend was a future vice-president, and in Albuquerque it was Billy the Kid. Life was colorful and wild in New Mexico and Elfego will embrace it fully for the rest of his life.

A newspaper editor and proprietor of the *Socorro Sun*, A.[Anthony] M. Conklin, arrived sometime in the summer of 1880 from the *Las Vegas Herald*. Conklin was originally born and raised in either Illinois or Indiana. He came to Socorro with obvious eastern Anglo-American ideals. Along with the addition of the train stop in Socorro, the peaceful small town had begun to change and grow, and with the newly arriving Anglos conflict with the original Hispanic citizens was unavoidable. The politicians, the old guard and newcomers, had different ideas about the growth and direction of the community, sometimes fueled by the newspaper.

On August 7, 1880, several months after his arrival to Socorro, A.M. Conklin wrote an editorial titled "Harmony" in the *Socorro Sun*:

> Socorro, August 7. – The one essential, the foundation stone, on which must be reared the prosperity of a town or a state is harmony. A spirit of contention will drive out enterprise and cripple prosperity. Let it be once known that any town is convulsed by internal dissensions. The better classes from other communities will pass it by, and only those who hate order, peace and good fellowship will come into it.

These few observations are not amiss just now and the property owners, the businessmen, those who have something at stake, something to lose by internal trouble, should see to it that those who stir up strife are summarily suppressed.

The men who wish to make trouble are usually men of no means and no character, who have nothing to lose, and the better classes of community should see that evil doers are required to cease from trouble.

While Conklin's editorial talks about harmony, the not-so-subtle use of the term 'better classes' cannot be mistaken. Conklin pens another article in the same paper editorializing the upcoming election process:

Socorro, August 7. – When the Republicans of this county determined to hold a convention, a half a dozen notices were written out in Spanish and posted up and as a consequence but few persons attended the convention. The Democrat territorial convention meets in Santa Fe next Monday, but so far as can be learned no convention has been called in this county.

This kind of convention is not just exactly up to the standard the new men has [sic] been used to and they will doubtless exercise their own judgment about supporting the nominees.

> Certainly any man with the sense and spirit necessary to constitute an intelligent voter will feel that he is not bound by the act of conventions in which he took no part.

In the politics of the time, Democrats, mostly Anglos, wanted to keep New Mexico as a territory for economic reasons. They aligned with business owners, who feared statehood would diminish their political power, and they demanded an English-only clause. Republicans, supported by *Nuevomexicanos*, objected to any English-only provision, believing there would be a natural evolution from Spanish to English with the influx of immigrants and natural growth of generations.

In the Sunday, September 25, 1880, *Socorro Sun*, A.M. Conklin wrote the following editorial:

> Socorro, September 25. – This paper has heretofore called attention to the importance of selecting the very best men in the county to fill the county offices at the approaching election. . . . Men are too often elected to offices for which they possess no special qualification and after they are in office take no steps to qualify themselves.
>
> In this rapidly growing community the officials should understand both the Spanish and English languages and it is not too much to say that a man who has the natural ability to fill an office would have learned the English language at least sufficiently to talk it in the thirty

years since the territory became a part of the United States. For the office of the County Commissioner one of the very best businessmen in the county should be selected. No other officers possess such powers untied to such a variety of duties, as do the members of the county Board. Men should be elected who possess a judicious liberality and will aid in building bridges, opening roads, establishing new precincts where needed so that the growth of the county may be accelerated.

It is an encouraging sign of the times, that the voters are exhibiting signs of independence and at the same time good men, worthy and well qualified are announcing themselves for office without waiting for party conventions to attach the brand of regularity to their candidacy. This gives promise of furnishing voters a chance to select good men and not to compelled to vote for any one merely because he is a choice of a party convention.

It is again fairly obvious that A.M. Conklin was a Democrat, promoting English-speaking candidates over *Nuevomexicano* Republican candidates. Obviously the election in the fall of 1880 was hotly contested between the original Hispanic settlers and newcomers, such as A.M. Conklin. The newcomers were anxious to change Socorro, to take over the local government, and to push the

Hispanics to the rear-of-the-bus. It is likely racial tensions were high in Socorro as 1880 came to an end.

The Bacas, along with other prominent Hispanic families, had been in New Mexico for hundreds of years and in the Socorro area for over a hundred. This was their land. They had built it out of the dirt and buried their dead in the same dirt. These families were the *Dons*, the Spanish knights and nobility of the area. These were not *peóns* [peasants], however many of the incoming immigrants did not care. To the newcomers, they were Mexicans, 'greasers,' when in reality the Hispanics were the natives of the area and all were now Americans under the Treaty of Guadalupe Hidalgo.

Onofre Baca was Elfego's older brother and for an unknown reason he did not move to Topeka with his family. He was left behind in Socorro. Onofre lived with his Uncle Gregorio Baca and Aunt Maria Demetria Torres, and his cousin Abrán in Socorro. Onofre was about six when the family left for Topeka, so he and his older cousin Abrán would have bonded as brothers as they grew up. The 1880 census showed Onofre as 'son' of Gregorio and Maria. Little is known of his youth or whether Elfego had much contact while in Topeka, but it can be assumed that once Elfego returned to Socorro, he and Onofre became reacquainted as brothers.

On Christmas Eve of 1880 a scuffle between Anglos and the Bacas turned into murder. This murder would affect Elfego and start a chain of events in Socorro. Animosity between Anglos and Hispanics ran both ways. A.M. Conklin, the editor of the *Socorro Sun* newspaper, was killed. Whether he was a specific target or just the victim of an unfortunate incident is not known:

> On that night, three members of the Baca clan, Antonio, Abrán and Onofre,

visited the church. When the Baca boys began to harass the young woman who sat in front of them, usher A.M. Conklin, editor of the Socorro Sun, asked them to leave. The trio walked out the door, but waited outside for Conklin. In gunfire exchanged when the last Christmas carol had been sung, Conklin was killed by the second bullet fired by Onofre Baca.[54]

The amount of misinformation and wrong information about this event is probably typical of this era, and will therefore be pointed out. The above passage from the book, *The Incident of New Mexico's Nightriders* by Bob L'Aloge, identifies the shooter as Onofre, Elfego's brother, which may later be disproved.

The *Daily New Mexican* newspaper in Santa Fe gave the following account of the tragedy in the December 28, 1880, edition titled "A Foul Murder," but failed to mention the three suspected assailants. The account in this article reads as if Jacobo Baca was the assailant:

Socorro, December 28. – Editor Conklin Falls by the Assassin's Hand. The people of the town of Socorro were horrified Friday night by the occurrence of a most brutal and cowardly murder in their town, of which the victim was A. M. Conklin, editor and proprietor of the Socorro Sun. Special dispatches to the New Mexican give the details of the affair as follow:

On the night of Christmas eve the Methodist church had a festival and a

Xmas tree for the benefit of the little ones. Mr. Conklin was appointed and acted as an usher and assistant to the ladies superintending the distribution of the presents. During the evening Jacobo Baca, a resident of Socorro and a rather prominent man, entered the church with his family, and having seated them in one part, walked over to the other side and took up a position immediately behind a young lady seated on one of the benches, placing his foot on the bench and in doing so trampling a shawl belonging to the lady which lay by her side. Mr. Conklin passed by, saw that Baca was soiling the shawl, and requested him to remove his foot. Baca paid no attention to the admonition. A second time he was asked to take his foot down, and again paying no attention to the request, Mr. Conklin removed the foot himself and picking up the shawl returned it to the owner. Baca immediately left the church.

   The festival came to an end at eleven o'clock and Mr. Conklin, with his wife on his arm, started home. As he stepped outside the door he was seized by a Mexican and drawn to one side, whom he grappled with. Baca, who had evidently been lying in wait, at this instant fired at Conklin but missed him. Seeing the flash, Conklin sprang at Baca who fired another shot, the bullet piercing Conklin's heart. He dropped and died instantly, while his wife dropped beside him in a dead faint. Baca fled and had not been found up to last night. There being no justice of the peace in Socorro, no warrant has been issued for the murderer, but miners and citizens are after him. The excitement in Socorro and the vicinity is at fever heat.

Author's Note: Referencing articles and information in this text which may be non-factual, but concerns the event is a deliberate attempt to show how the misinformation of the time may have fueled other events. It has also been noted by the author that the newspapers of the time were consistently error-prone due to the nature of verbal stories and accounts, which would have made misspellings and misinformation problematic.

Resentment and animosity was escalating in Socorro. As the newspaper article stated, "the excitement in Socorro and the vicinity is at fever heat."

Charles Montgomery reported in the *Journal of American Ethnic History*, that Conklin and the Bacas had a rocky history:

As editor of the Socorro Sun, Conklin was an aggressive critic of the Baca's politic influence, and his writing had magnified the distrust between Socorro's Spanish-speaking majority and the area's English-speaking newcomers.[55]

Several accounts assumed the young Baca men deliberately went to the Methodist Church to find Conklin and start trouble or murder him. But, the Gregorio Bacas were not Catholic and belonged to Pastor Harwood's Methodist Church. This was their church and it was Christmas Eve.[56]

It was also suggested that the three young men had been out drinking, or were drunk before the incident, and they instigated the conflict against the newspaper editor on purpose:

> But whiskey is no reason for murder. So these three young hidalgos had to find an excuse for their dastardly deed. They must create a situation, in their opinion, that would justify the murder of Socorro's editor. Then they could silence him and his "gringo" newspaper for good. The code of the olden Spanish-hidalgo was such that they felt they were above others . . . Better than the peons who roamed about the streets in search of a living. A fine excuse could be found if they could get the gringo Conklin to insult them in some way.[57]

The theory A.M. Conklin was an intentional target is unlikely. There would have been ways to silence or intimidate the editor in a much less public and anonymous way. The young lady involved in the incident was not A.M. Conklin's wife, and the editor was just coincidentally acting as an usher. Why attempt a murder in such a public way against an unarmed man? These young men made no attempt to hide their identities; everyone knew them. Convicted murderers were hung in 1880, so would these three shooters risk this type of confrontation in a public place? Was it likely these men would risk their lives in this way? It seems more likely that tempers boiled, followed by the exchange of words and bullets.

Pastor Harwood's annual reports to the Methodist Church states that he was fluent in both English and Spanish. He started his pastoral career in 1858 and opened a number of Methodist Churches and Spanish schools in the area. Both Hispanics and Anglos belonged to Pastor Thomas Harwood's church.

Original Methodist Church circa 1880s in Socorro, New Mexico, where A.M. Conklin was shot and killed on December 24, 1880. Photograph reproduction courtesy of the Socorro Historical Society.

Abrán and Onofre were raised as brothers by Gregorio Baca. The third assailant, Antonio Baca, was Gregorio's younger brother and uncle to the two boys. Born in 1856, he was a year or two older than Abrán and Onofre. Antonio and Gregorio's mother and father are listed as Methodists, joining Reverend Harwood's church in 1873.[58] The three young men no doubt joined Gregorio, Maria, and their grandparents and possibly other relatives and friends for the church service on Christmas Eve. It seems unlikely this was a venue they might have plotted murder. All the accounts of the evening of Christmas Eve 1880 assume the Bacas were visiting the church or deliberately barging into the church service, perhaps to cause trouble, when the reality was they were attending Christmas Eve service at their own church with their family.

Onofre [standing] and Abrán Baca, Socorro, New Mexico. Exact date of photograph is not known, but assumed to be shortly before the disastrous events of 1880. Photograph courtesy of the private collection of Mary Baca Aguilar, family relative of Elfego Baca, Socorro, New Mexico.

Abrán, Antonio, and Onofre were part of a large and well respected family. They would have been raised with the best Socorro had to offer. Antonio, Abrán, and Onofre were sons of the Socorro Baca families, who owned one of New Mexico's biggest mercantile businesses. Did they feel they were above the law or that the community would unite to protect them in this killing, or were they just three young men with too many hormones and too much *bravado* and tired of being harassed?

> The Bacas were members of "an old megatherium [sic] family whose traditions and ripeness were time-honored before Coronado stepped into history. Of royal vintage," writes Father Stanley, "they played a tremendous part in colonizing and settling of New Mexico, to the very days of the Santa Fe Trail, the invasion of the Texans [and] the march of Americans . . . They were prominent in Socorro from the very beginning. Their escutcheon was to be found with every Conquistador who sallied forth from Mexico City in the name of the Crown and Christianity. They were hildagos [sic], peacemakers, Indian-fighters, Conquistadors striking tap-roots along the trail, permeating the country with Spanish culture, Spanish pride, and Spanish trade."[59]

The use of the term, *hidalgo*, by L'Aloge in *The Incident of New Mexico's Nightriders*, also confirms the Baca families were considered noblemen or very prominent in the community at the time. Their ancestor, Captain Cristóbal Baca and his lineage, earned this distinction in the early 1600s. Certainly the Bacas were one of the founding families of Socorro. They were land owners and businessmen. The founding Baca families, these *hidalgos*, had been land owners in New Mexico for over two hundred years. The extended family was active in the community, church, and politics in the area. You could label them 'the old guard.' It is certain these young men, Antonio, Abrán, and Onofre were not street ruffians. Perhaps they were defending their life and land from the invaders, just as their ancestors defended against the Moors.

Blood Will Be Spilled

The death of Conklin only made matters worse in Socorro between Anglos and Hispanic residents. The town constable, Juan Maria Garcia, a relative of the Bacas, refused to arrest the young men. His inaction infuriated the Anglo population. So the day after Conklin's death, Colonel Ethan Eaton, a former Civil War soldier, formed a lynch mob, a group of citizen vigilantes and conveniently named it 'Socorro Committee of Safety.' The so-called committee demanded all citizens in Socorro to support them, increasing the animosity between the two cultures. The vigilantes took action:

> The day after Christmas angry by the inaction of sheriff Juan Maria Garcia, Col. Ethan W. Eaton, prominent Socorro rancher, organized a vigilante committee to force sheriff Garcia to lead them to the Baca hacienda at the south end of town.[60]

Author's Note: In some accounts of Eaton's vigilante action to arrest the Bacas, the sheriff was named Garcia and in other cases it was Montoya. It is unknown which name is correct, but both law men, if these were different men, refused. The names used in the following accounts are as given in the references. Newspaper reporting at the time was verbal, and mistakes in spelling and specifics were common.

On Monday December 27, 1880, Colonel Eaton and his band of vigilantes surrounded the house of newly-elected Sheriff Montoya and demanded he arrest the Bacas. Sheriff Montoya refused. Eaton had obtained an arrest warrant issued by Justice Blackman to arrest the Bacas, and when Montoya refused, Eaton and the vigilantes arrested Montoya and eight other Hispanics. Montoya was arrested for 'dereliction of duty' and the eight Hispanics were arrested for 'aiding the criminals to escape.' The sheriff and the eight men were taken to the Park Hotel and were guarded by two hundred heavily armed men. Justice in Socorro had been taken over by mob rule.

On Tuesday, December 28, ex-sheriff, Juan Garcia, Vigil Garcia, and Antonio Abeytia approached Colonel Eaton and demanded him to release the prisoners. Eaton declined:

> The Mexicans then said that unless their demand was complied with, they would exterminate the Americans. But the Americans are firm. They are determined to hold their prisoners until the murderers are given up. The Mexicans have been given until four o'clock this afternoon to answer, and if not complied with they threaten the lives of the hostages. So far the Mexicans have shown no indication to comply, and it is anticipated that BLOOD WILL BE SPILLED tonight.[61]

As is typical of writings from this time period, the term 'Americans' meant Anglo-Americans and 'Mexicans' meant any Hispanic or mixed-race persons. This disregarded the fact that all of the residents of New Mexico had been granted citizen rights by the Treaty of Guadalupe Hidalgo in 1848 and many had been in the territory for longer periods of time than the newcomers.

The Baca family, Elfego's ancestors, had survived the hardships of colonizing New Spain's Kingdom of New Mexico since their arrival in 1600. Was it any wonder they resented the dismissive treatment by the newcomers?

Colonel Eaton sent word out to the mining communities and cattle ranches in the county asking Americans to come to Socorro to fight Mexicans.

Author's Note: Colonel Eaton and the vigilantes referred to and considered any Hispanics in the area, Mexicans, and the use of the term Mexican in this section is from their perspective.

The telegram sent by Colonel Eaton sent at 9:55 a.m. on December 28, to San Marcial read:

> City marshal of San Marcial — Send immediately as many Americans, well armed, as you have to save the lives of the Americans at SOCORRO.[62]

San Marcial City Marshal, H. Hill, immediately telegraphed, A. Robinson, division superintendent, for permission to take engine no. 97. Robinson denied permission, nevertheless, thirty-five American vigilantes commandeered the train engine and arrived in Socorro.

Later that day Eaton and his vigilantes approached a house where they believed the Bacas were hiding. There were about sixty Mexicans guarding the house, and Eaton brought about two hundred vigilantes including Sheriff Montoya. War was about to break out in Socorro.

Sheriff Montoya was fearful for his life from both sides. Eaton told him to talk to the people in the house and ask if the Bacas where there. From inside, the reply was, "no," the Bacas were not there. Eaton told the sheriff to tell the people that if they didn't come out, they would dynamite the place to the ground.

When the door opened, Antonio and Abrán made a break for their horses. The vigilantes chased and caught Antonio, but Abrán fled and headed to Mexico. There was no sign of Onofre.

Santa Fe's *Daily New Mexican*, December 29, 1880, ran an account of the arrest of Antonio, titled "Great Excitement Existing," by Special Dispatch to the *New Mexican*:

> Socorro, December 29. – The whole trouble at this place has been caused by Sheriff Baca's refusing to act in arresting the murderer of Conklin who is a relative of his. Sheriff Baca, Antonio Baca and three other Mexicans were arrested yesterday by the citizens and placed under guard. Antonio Baca attempted to escape during the night and wounded one of the guards who killed him. The other four prisoners have been released on bail. This last killing has stirred up great indignation among the Mexicans and the excitement runs high. The most prominent of the Mexicans and Americans here are using all their efforts and influence to preserve the peace. Trouble is expected to-night as it is thought that the Mexicans are intending to avenge the death of Baca.

In the above article, the sheriff was named Baca, but in other accounts was Garcia or Montoya. It is believed the sheriff's name, as Baca, was confused as a relative of the

Bacas, which accounts for the incorrect naming of the sheriff.

Antonio was arrested and put in jail in Socorro. Colonel Eaton made sure his prisoner was heavily guarded. He had one of the Bacas and he made sure the prisoner would not escape. Later that same day, Deputy Jack Ketcham entered Antonio's cell. The prisoner had somehow obtained a pistol and fired at Ketcham hitting him in the side. Ketcham drew his six-shooter and fired killing Antonio Baca.

The *Las Vegas Daily Optic* headlines for December 29, 1880, read:

> AT SOCORRO! Baca, One of the Murderers of Conklin, Captured and Placed in Jail. He is Handed a Revolver from the Outside, Shoots a Guard, Who Kills Him. The Excitement Subsiding and All Serious Trouble Thought to Be at an End.

It is hard to believe, if Antonio was heavily guarded, how could anyone easily get a gun to him. Could it be the vigilantes didn't want to waste a rope on Antonio Baca? It may have been politically correct at the time to kill him attempting to escape and circumvent a trial. In another account about Antonio's death, it was believed Antonio was held in a room at the Park Hotel. Antonio's sister supposedly smuggled a gun to him and he attempted to breakout and was shot and killed:

> Antonio Baca was taken and was held at the Park Hotel under armed guard. Two days later Antonio's sister smuggled

a gun and he attempted to breakout and was shot and killed after wounding the guard.[63]

In either case, the vigilantes were happy. One of the Bacas was dead. The capture and subsequent death of Antonio Baca was the first act of the Socorro Committee of Safety or Socorro vigilantes. On January 1, 1881, the *Socorro Sun* newspaper ran the following proclamation:

> NOTICE — To all whom it may concern. Notice is hereby given that all violations of peace and good order by any person or persons irrespective of nationality or condition will be meritably followed by speedy and sure punishment, By order of S.C. of S.

The proclamation was printed in both English and Spanish and marked the beginning of the Socorro Committee of Safety, or S.C.of S. Its reign of power lasted a little over three years.

Much to the anger of the vigilantes, two of the perpetrators had escaped capture: Abrán and Onofre. Colonel Eaton and his vigilante leaders convinced Governor W. G. Ritch to offer a reward for the capture of the Bacas. On January 10, 1881, the governor posted a $250 reward for their capture. Colonel Eaton believed the Bacas had escaped to Ysleta, Texas, and he hoped the reward would prompt officials or bounty hunters to go after them. The WANTED posters made their way across New Mexico, Arizona, and into Texas.

A Texas Ranger named James B. Gillett knew the Bacas had an uncle, Judge Jose Baca, living in Ysleta, Texas. Gillett posted a man to watch for activity at the uncle's house. His man finally spotted two young Mexican men sitting on the porch. Gillett gathered some of his ranger friends and arrested the two men.

Gillett documents that Jose Baca attempted to bribe him. The posted reward for the two outlaws was $500. He reported the Judge offered him up to $1,000 for Gillett to walk away. Gillett refused.[64]

On February 27, 1881, Gillett escorted the prisoners to Socorro and in March Abrán Baca was held for trial, but the other man was not Onofre. He was Merrias Baca who was then released. Abrán was later relocated to a jail in Santa Fe for his safety until such time as the court could be convened.

The *Daily New Mexican*, March 1, 1881, ran an account of the arrest of Abrán Baca, titled "All Quiet," by Special Dispatch to the *New Mexican*:

> Socorro, March 1. – Abran and Mimais [Merrias] Baca, the two murderers of A. M. Conklin, are here and in jail. All question as to their identity is settled, as they have been recognized by several people. A strong guard has been placed around the jail, but there appears to be no excitement here, and there is no cause to apprehend trouble.

Onofre was still at large. Around March of 1881 Santiago Cooper contacted Ranger Gillett, telling him of a man fitting the description of Onofre Baca, who was working at a store in Saragosa [Zaragoza], Mexico, a town about ten miles south of El Paso. Gillett paid Cooper $25 to go to Zaragoza and make sure the young man was Onofre. Cooper returned in about a week verifying that it was Onofre. Disregarding international law, Gillett and another ranger crossed the river and apprehended Baca:

> I planned to attempt the capture of Baca the next morning and send Cooper back to Saragosa [Zaragoza] to look over the situation there once more. He informed me on his return that Baca was still clerking in the store. I now told Lloyd to keep our horses up when the animals were turned out to graze next morning. This move caused no especial [sic] comment, for the men frequently would keep their horses to ride down town. As soon as we had crossed the Rio Grande into Mexico I planned to quit the public road, travel through the bosques, pass around the west side of Saragosa and ride quickly up to the store in which our man was working. Lloyd was to hold the horses while I was to dismount, enter the store, and make the arrest. Then, if possible, I was to mount Baca behind Lloyd and make a quick getaway.
>
> Our plans were carried out almost to the letter. We reached Saragosa safely, and while Lloyd held my horse in front of the store I entered and discovered Baca measuring some goods for an old Mexican woman. I stepped up to him, seized him by the collar, and with drawn pistol ordered him to come with me. The customer promptly fainted and fell to the

floor. Two other people ran from the building, screaming at the top of their voices. Baca hesitated about going with me, and in broken English asked where he was to be taken. I informed him to Paso del Norte, and, shoving my pistol against his head, ordered him to step lively. When we reached our horses I made him mount behind Lloyd. I then jumped into my saddle and, waving my pistol over my head, we left Saragosa on a dead run.

As I left Saragosa I saw men getting their horses together and knew that in a few minutes a posse would be following us. When we had gone two miles almost at top speed I saw Lloyd's horse was failing, and we lost a little time changing Baca to my mount. We had yet two miles to go, most of the way through deep sand. I could see a cloud of dust, and shortly a body of mounted men hove in view. It was a tense moment. Lloyd thought it was all off with us, but we still had a long lead and our horses were running easily. As our pursuers made a bend in the road we counted nine men in the group. When they had drawn up within six hundred yards they began firing on us. This was at long range and did no damage. In fact, I believe they were trying to frighten rather than to wound us, as they were just as likely to hit Baca as either of us. We reached the Rio Grande at last, and while it was almost one hundred yards wide it was flat and shallow at the ford. We hit the water running, and as I mounted the bank on good old Texas soil I felt like one who has made a home run in a world series baseball game. Our pursuers halted at the river, so I pulled off my hat, waved to them, and disappeared up the road.[65]

Gillett's writing of the event reads like a bad western fiction novel. He forgot to have his horse rear back on two legs, like 'the Lone Ranger's *hi-ho* Silver,' as he reenters 'good old Texas.' Riding double on a horse is hard enough on both the riders and horse, and outrunning a posse is unbelievable. Keeping an untied Baca on the horse while being chased — well, you decide.

Is Gillett's version the real account of the event? Gillett's version differs greatly from an account reported in the *Cheyenne Transporter* newspaper in 1881 and was also refuted in L'Aloge's *The Incident of New Mexico's Nightriders*. L'Aloge paraphrases the memoir's of Chester D. Potter published in the *Pittsburgh[PA] Dispatch*. In this article, Gillett apprehended Onofre at his wedding during the evening's dance, not at the store:

> Satisfied as to Baca's whereabouts, he took another ranger, by the name of Robinson, and the two leading a third horse, saddled and bridled, forded the Rio Grande and started after the man. They [the Rangers] timed their ride so

as to arrive at the Mexican village early in the evening. Inquiry developed not only the fact that Baca was there, but also, the complicating feature that he had been married that day, and that the baille [dance], always held in celebration of a Mexican nuptial contract, was then in full blast at the home of the bride.

They rode up to the adobe in which the wedding dance was on, and asked for Baca. Some of the men outside told them he was dancing but that they should come right in and join the festivities. Gillette [sic] declined, and asked them to inform Baca that two friends were outside with a very important message for him.[66]

Baca rushed out of the dance at the wrong end of their six-shooters. At gunpoint, Baca mounted the third horse and was spirited away in the night.

In the *Cheyenne Transporter* of April 25, 1881, an article titled "Two Days Married" about the arrest of Onofre Baca was published. The story supports the fact that Baca was abducted from his wedding:

> Socorro, April 25. – Enofrio [Onofre] Baca, the murderer of Conklin, has had a career which reminds one of that of Solomon Grundy, the fastest man on record. Baca grew up not so rapidly, to be sure, as Grundy, but recently he has made almost as good time as that noted character of nursery fame. At Serigosa,

New Mexico [Zaragosa, Mexico], two days before his capture by Sergeant Gillette, of the Texas Rangers, Baca took unto himself a wife, selected from among the handsomest senoritas of Old Mexico's first families. The ceremony was witnessed by his mother and father, who were present to witness the happiness of their boy murderer. The wedding was attended by a number of the friends of the young lady, and there was feasting and merry-making on the important occasion. But Sergeant Gillette put in an appearance, and a change came over the spirit of the young man's dream. He was conveyed to Deming, whither he was accompanied by his parents, and thence to San Marcial, where the party got off and took a freight for Socorro, possibly for the purpose of avoiding an angry mob, which might have met them at the depot at the end of the journey. Early next morning he was taken out of jail and hung. On Saturday he was married, on Monday he was captured, on Thursday he was hung and Friday buried. Baca said on his way up from Mexico that he expected to be lynched as soon as he got home, and he was right.

The reference in this article in regards to 'his mother and father' would have been Gregorio and Maria, his aunt and uncle who raised him.

Gillett recalls when they got back to camp, Lieutenant Baylor ordered Gillett to let Baca go free. Gillett refused, saying, "I have been with the Texas Rangers for six years, and I have seen many murderers go free because they crossed over into Mexico. This time I had to take the law into my own hands."

However, Lieutenant Baylor relented and allowed Gillett to turn Baca over and collect his $500 reward. Mexico vigorously protested the Gillett invasion and the kidnapping of Baca. Washington D. C. officials put pressure on Texas Governor Oran M. Roberts to force Gillett to resign from the rangers, which he did, on December 26, 1881. Gillett's deed across the international border of Mexico, to apprehend Onofre, was an illegal act which cost Onofre his life.

The following account in James B. Gillett's book, *Six Years with the Texas Rangers 1875 – 1881,* details Gillett's trip to return Onofre to New Mexico and the actions of the vigilantes and how a large mob undermined justice:

> On the following day we reached Rincon, then the terminus of the Santa Fe Railroad. I had wired the officers of Socorro from El Paso that I had captured Baca and was on my way to New Mexico with him. Baca's friends had also been informed of arrest, and they lost no time in asking the governor of New Mexico to have me bring the prisoner to Santa Fe, as they feared mob violence at Socorro. When I reached San Martial [Marcial] I was handed a telegram from the governor ordering me to bring Baca to

Santa Fe, and on no account to stop with him in Socorro.

Because of delay on the railroad I did not reach Socorro until late at night. The minute the train stopped it was boarded by twenty-five or thirty armed men, headed by Deputy Sheriff [Colonel] Eaton. I showed Eaton the governor's telegram, but he declared Baca was wanted at Socorro and that was where he was going. I remonstrated with him and declared I was going on to Santa Fe with the prisoner. By this time a dozen armed men had gathered around me who declared, "Not much will you take him to Santa Fe." I was furious, but I was practically under arrest and powerless to help myself. Baca and I were transferred from the train to a big bus that was in waiting. The jailer entered first, then Baca was seated next to him, and I sat next the door with my Winchester in my hand. The driver was ordered to drive to the jail.

It was a bright moonlight night and we had not traveled far up the street when I looked out and saw at least a hundred armed men. They came from every direction. The men swarmed around the bus and three or four of them grabbed the horses by the bridle reins, while others tried to force open the doors. I asked the jailer if I could depend on him to help me stand the mob off, but he replied it would do no good. I was now madder than ever, and for the first time in my life I ripped out an oath, saying, "Goddamn them, I am going to stand them off!"

As the doors were forced I poked my Winchester out and ordered the mob to stand back or I would shoot. The men paid no more attention to my gun than if it had been a broomstick. A man standing beside the bus door seized the muzzle and, with a quick jerk to one side, caused it to fly out of my hand and out upon the ground. Another man grabbed me by the collar and proceeded to pull me out of the bus. I spread my legs and tried to brace myself, but a hard and quick jerk landed me out on the ground, where one of the men kicked me. I was tame now, and made no effort to draw my pistol. One of the crowd said to me, "What in hell do you mean? We do not wish to hurt you but we are going to hang that damned Mexican right now!" I then informed the mob of the nature of Baca's arrest and told them that the hanging of the prisoner would place me in an awkward position. Then, too, the reward offered by the territory of New Mexico was for the delivery of the murderer inside the jail doors of Socorro County. The leaders of the crowd consulted for a few minutes and then concluded I was right. They ordered me back into the bus, gave me my Winchester, and we all started for the jail. As soon as Baca had been placed in prison Deputy Sheriff [Colonel] Eaton sat down and wrote a receipt for the delivery of Baca inside the jail doors. By this time day was beginning to break and I tried to stay the hanging by making another talk. The mob interpreted my motive and invited me to step down a block to their community room where they would talk with me. I started with them but we had gone only a hundred yards when the whole mob broke back to the jail. T [sic] started to go with them but two men held me, saving, "It's no use; they are going to hang him."

  The men took Baca to a nearby corral and hanged him to a big beam of the gate. The next morning Baca's relatives came to me at the hotel with hats in their hands and asked me for the keys with which to remove the shackles from the dead man's legs. As I handed them the keys I felt both mortified and ashamed. A committee of citizen sat Socorro waited on me just before I took the train for home, counted out $250 as their part of the reward, and thanked me for capturing the two murderers.[67]

Unquestionably Gillett knew of the situation in Socorro and Colonel Eaton's vigilantes. However, he was a lawman or a bounty hunter taking a suspected murderer to stand trial, although, he stated he was ashamed of the actions. Onofre Baca, Elfego's brother, was lynched the night of March 30 or early the morning of March 31, 1881.

The Baca relatives who came for the keys to Onofre's shackles, as so noted in Gillett's passage, would most likely have been the Baca men, Gregorio, Abdenago, and very possibly Elfego. Francisco Baca, father of Onofre and Elfego, was sitting in a jail cell in Los Lunas. One can only assume the bitterness for the vigilantes was deeply ingrained in young sixteen-year-old Elfego.

While certainly not faultless, the three assailants of A.M. Conklin received less than justice. Antonio was killed, presumably trying to escape from jail. Onofre was lynched. Abrán was brought back to Socorro from Santa Fe to stand trial in November 1881. The prosecution's case was weak, and three of the major witnesses failed to show up at court. By all accounts it is believed that Antonio Baca was the one who actually shot A.M. Conklin in a moment of rage. Abrán was found not guilty. Abrán, fearing the wrath of the vigilantes, leaped out of the courthouse window to a waiting horse and fled out of town. Ironically, Onofre may have been released also, if he had lived, but the mob had ruled, not the law.[68]

The lynch mob of vigilantes, Socorro Committee of Safety, ruled Socorro until 1884, lynching at least five men, maybe more, and threatened many others. The vigilantes included local bankers, lawyers, and businessmen determined to 'clean up the town,' and even though the mob wore masks, everyone knew who they were. Although it was not sanctioned by any law, the committee acted as the law for three years. The committee forcibly took the law into its own hands. Lynchings, whippings, and intimidation stoked the tensions in the community of Socorro to a fevered pitch.

Elfego was living in Socorro and sixteen years old when his brother Onofre was lynched by the vigilantes in1881. Although Elfego does not address the lynching in his autobiographies, one can assume the entire Baca clan, as well as the Hispanic community in Socorro, was deeply affected by the arrest and killing of Antonio and the vigilante lynching of Onofre. Young Elfego was thrust into an incredible education of 'justice' in his hometown. The entire situation must have instilled in him how American law can sometimes be overruled by mob law.

Elfego Stands Tall

The vigilantes search for and subsequent lynching of Elfego's brother, Onofre, was not the only family matter affecting young Elfego in the spring of 1881. He turned sixteen in February of that year, barely a man, while at the same time growing up quickly. It is not clear from his writings where he was living or what he was doing during this period, but Elfego had plenty of relatives in the area, uncles, cousins, and grandparents, or he may have been in Albuquerque with Billy the Kid. Albuquerque, Belen, and Socorro are all within a short ride or he could have hopped a train car.

According to Elfego, when his father Francisco returned to Socorro, he was hired as the Town Marshal for the town of Belen in Valencia County. Belen is located about thirty miles south of Albuquerque, about half-way to Socorro. He also purchased a quarter horse. Francisco may have acquired keen knowledge about racehorses and racing from the Charles Curtis family in North Topeka.

Sometime in late 1880, Francisco was horse racing in the Belen or nearby Los Lunas area. Apparently, his horse won, much to the dismay of a prominent Los Lunas family:

> His [Elfego's] career began rather auspiciously a year later upon the return of his father and subsequent assuming by the gentleman of the role of Town Marshal of Belen. Father Baca was also of sporting enough inclinations to possess a quarter horse that very rudely shattered the hopes of a prominent citizen of Los Lunas, a powerful family in

the state of New Mexico. The shattering was followed by words and combat that led to the gentleman returning to Los Lunas with his face bashed into strange and curious contour. Father Baca, fresh from the freedom of Kansas, was not of a type to admire the gentleman from Los Lunas. His words to that effect and his rude usage of the gentleman were considered very gravely in the councils of the great family and placed carefully in the black books of the clan.[69]

Sometime after the fracas with the Los Lunas family, Marshal Francisco Baca was called to deal with a disturbance at the Fredrick Scholle & Company in Belen. The call was about a fight inside the store. The Santa Fe *Daily New Mexican* reported on Monday, December 27, 1880:

> Socorro, December 27. – A party of drunken Mexicans got into a row . . . in the store of F[redrick] Scholle & Co. Pistols were drawn and a policeman, Francisco Baca y Volarde started in to stop the row. The drunken men pitched into the officer and he fired into the crowd, killing Eutimino Baca and wounding Termino Baca, a brother of Eutimino.

The article above reported the two drunken men as, Eutimino and Termino Baca. Their actual names were

Otimio and Saturnino Baca, and they were not related to the Francisco Baca clan.

Saturnino died a few days later from his wounds. The killing was a few days after Christmas in 1880, a few days after Elfego's brother, Onofre, was involved in killing A.M. Conklin in Socorro. His father was not immediately arrested for the killing. However, on February 2, 1881, Francisco Baca was arrested for the event and charged with murder.

Although this event occurred in Belen, it has to be considered that the Socorro vigilante sentiments against the Bacas were raging. Belen is only about forty miles north of Socorro. Surely the vigilante opinions would have been the talk of the area. Elfego's father was an appointed Town Marshal, who was dispatching his job. Why then should he be arrested and tried for murder?

Santa Fe's *Daily New Mexican* reported Francisco's arrest and conviction on February 2, 1881:

> Socorro, February 2. – Francisco Baca was arrested and taken to jail in Los Lunas, the Valencia county seat. Francisco was tried at district court in May and found guilty of murder in the fifth degree in one of the killings. He was sentenced to a prison term and because there was no territorial prisons in New Mexico, Francisco had to stay in the Los Lunas jail until he could be transported to the Kansas state prison.

Elfego felt the harsh sentence was a trumped-up injustice against his father. He believed the powerful Los Lunas family [horseracing incident in December of 1880] was behind the arrest and the guilty verdict against Francisco.

By mid spring of 1881 his brother Onofre had been lynched, his uncle Antonio killed by the vigilantes, his cousin Abrán was in jail in Santa Fe awaiting trial for murder, and his father had been convicted of murder in Los Lunas. Gone were the days of youthful innocence. The adult Elfego, the man afraid of no one, was about to emerge in Socorro.

Young Elfego formulated a plan to break his father out of jail in Los Lunas. Around June 24, 1881, Elfego and a friend, known only by the name of Chávez, traveled to Los Lunas on foot. Elfego planned the breakout on a day the Catholic Church was having a fiesta. Elfego and his friend Chávez waited for the jailer to leave the jailhouse to attend mass. Elfego knew the jailer would go directly to the fiesta after mass:

> They found the jail on the first floor of a rambling two-storied adobe which housed the court room as a second floor. The cell of Father Baca lay directly beneath the second floor room to which the jury retired for deliberations. Elfego went around to the placitas at the rear of the structure and secured a ladder used for window washing. Placing it against the side the court house and jail, he ascended to the jury room, crept through the easily opened window, and proceeded, with the aid of Chavez, to saw out a space in the floor large enough for the body of Father Baca to wiggle through from beneath. It was

leisurely work. The jailer was gone for the night; it was midnight and they were too far from the habitations of Los Lunas to occasion suspicion by the sawing. They sawed until the last board creaked through and they could see Father Baca waiting patiently below.

Two fellow prisoners boosted Father Baca through the opening and were in turn boosted and yanked through to freedom. With this done, there was ample time to think of making a getaway. Young Elfego returned the ladder politely to its place in the placitas and spent such time as was necessary in stripping the clothes line of the jailer of the jerked venison hanging thereon. With it came ears of corn and chili — food enough for a fair-sized cavalcade. Amply stocked, the five — Father Baca, and the two other prisoners, Elfego and Young Chavez — walked calmly across the road to a clump of high grass approximately seventy-five feet from the jail and courthouse entrance. The first faint rays of sun were struggling over the horizon. It was four o'clock in the morning.

In the high grass within easy access of the hubbub at the county jail, the five munched jerked meat, corn, chili and watermelons from the field they were lying in, and watched with considerable interest through the long day while the sheriff and deputy sheriffs and posses of great size and indignation started out from the jail entrance and beat the surrounding country with energy and abandon in search of the gentleman who had so grossly dishonored the stability of the Valencia County carcel. There were hullabaloos and shouts and strenuous flaunting of deadly weapons.

"The culprits," declared the stern voice of the sheriff which carried beautifully to the popeyed spectators in the high grass, "the culprits must be apprehended for the honor of good old Valencia County." Or words to that effect. The culprits wettened [sic] their faces with another bite of luscious Valencia County watermelon and nodded grave assent to the sheriff's determination. Determination was a part of a good sheriff's stock in trade. The culprits would have been chagrined to be outwitting the sheriff who had neither determination nor effectiveness. It was reasonably certain that he was to fall short in effectiveness. It was entirely necessary that he should retain determination.

It was rather a nice day for young Elfego. He had more to eat than was good for him, but he had the pleasure of checking out the posses as they left the jail and checking them in again as they returned, weary and a bit dejected, from scouring the mountains and beating up and down the banks of the silvery Rio Grande. The experience gained then was to be of service to him later when, as sheriff, he picked up criminals within earshot of the site of their crimes rather than credit them with airplane hops away from there. The average criminal, quoth [sic] Mr. Baca in his more mature years, is generally unable to get away rapidly from the scene of the devilment and wisely, is often unwilling to do same.

After dark the Baca picnicking party broke up and prepared for departure. The two fellow prisoners headed North for Albuquerque, Father Baca, Elfego and Young Chavez started South for Escondida, three miles north of the town of Socorro. At Escondida, they dropped Young Chavez and secured three horses and a guide who knew the way to Old Mexico. There was no rush now. They were in the bosom of their own family. There were uncles to the right of them, nephews to the left. At the first approach of a strange face, the community would have arisen in behalf of the Baca connection. At the end of four days, they proceeded on to Socorro, Texas, which was in turn but half of

> Socorro, Old Mexico. Father Baca spent a period of seven years with a brother who kept a store at Ysleta, Texas, near El Paso. He returned at the end of that time to be a respected citizen of his native country.[70]

Onofre Baca had headed to Ysleta, Texas or Zaragoza, Mexico wanting to escape the New Mexican law, and later his father followed on a similar route after Elfego broke him out of jail. These towns are all now part of the El Paso, Texas, and the Juárez, Mexico area. As the article indicates, they had a lot of friends and family in this area and would have been protected from the law. When the Spanish settlers of Santa Fe retreated during the Pueblo Revolt of the 1680s, the Baca family spent over a decade in the area before returning to New Mexico. Parts of the Baca family, no doubt, stayed and flourished in the El Paso area, as indicated by Elfego's use of the words 'bosom of their own family.' The El Paso area is also a major town just over the Texas border and would have been a likely choice for evading New Mexican authorities.

Apparently it was safe for Francisco to be in Texas and he stayed there for seven years. Why the law did not actively seek and find Francisco in Texas during these seven years is unknown. Ranger James Gillett had crossed the border to Mexico to apprehend Onofre, however no one seemed inclined to capture Francisco in Texas. Was it because the victims in the case of Francisco were Hispanics and A.M. Conklin was an Anglo inciting racial revenge?

In 1888 Francisco returned to New Mexico. No other information about Francisco is known: where he lived, when he returned to New Mexico, what he did, or when he died. He was approximately 55 years old in 1888.

The act of breaking his father out of jail showed both courage and a lack of self-concern in the sixteen-year-old Elfego. A Spanish daring rooted from his distant ancestors, such as Antonio Baca, when he and his anti-Rosas rebels fought against Governor Luis Rosas in Santa Fe in 1642, surfaced in Elfego. In the tradition of generations of Spanish citizenry, who would drop their plows, close their shops, and leave their classrooms to pick up arms to go to battle against the Moors, young Elfego saw injustice and acted.

What Elfego did after the jailbreak is unclear. One might expect he was afraid to return to Socorro for some time, even though there was no legal implication he was connected to the jailbreak. Perhaps it was not considered by the authorities that a boy of sixteen would attempt such a bold caper. Elfego gave no hints in either autobiography about this event. On June 26, 1881, the *Daily New Mexican* ran an article about the Los Lunas jailbreak under the headline "More Jail Birds Flown":

> Socorro, June 26. – A day or two ago the jail of Valencia County was broken and delivered of all the occupants save one poor unfortunate who through the treacherous conduct of his companions got left. The jail contained Francisco Baca, John Pearee [Pearce?], a man with the euphonious alias, Thacker, the wife murderer, and one or two other less famous criminals. . . . The jail at Los Lunas is built of stone but the ceiling consisted merely of inch boards, to cut through which was no difficult task.

No mention was made in the article of who might have aided the escapees. According to Elfego's account of the story, it was nighttime and no one would have seen either he or Chávez performing the daring deed.

What is known is that by the autumn of 1884 he was back and working for his uncle Jose Baca at the mercantile store in Socorro.

Life in Socorro

Sometime after the Los Lunas jailbreak, Elfego went to work in the family business at his Uncle Juan Jose Baca's large mercantile store in Socorro. In his autobiography he stated he was paid $20 a month and room and board. Elfego goes on to say, "At that time there was a whole lot of shooting and killing at Socorro." Socorro and Socorro County had a growing population, including miners and cattlemen.

Before the 1880s, Socorro was primarily a Hispanic town. Mrs. Sadie Abernathy was quoted as saying:

> "When I came to Socorro in 1876, the little town was a paradise. Lots of fruit trees, grape vines, (and) gardens . . . (There were) no groceries or dry good stores except for one run by J.J. Baca Sr."[71]

The J.J. Baca Sr. store referenced by Mrs. Abernathy was the Baca family store owned by Elfego's Uncle Juan Jose Baca. It sat on the north side of the plaza on the corner of Bernard and Abeyta Streets. The building still graces the Socorro Heritage Plaza, currently the home of an art gallery and bistro.

Jose Baca's [JJ Baca] store circa 1910. Photograph reproduction courtesy of the Socorro Historical Society.

In 1910, A.B. (Abdenago) Baca, Elfego's older brother, built a large family home about one block from the store, just off the plaza. It was a large home where many generations of Bacas have lived, been born, and died. Gilbert Baca, grandson of Abdenago Baca, owns the home today.

Baca family home, Socorro, New Mexico. Abdenago Baca standing on the porch in a white shirt. Photograph courtesy of the private collection of Gilbert Baca, grandson of Abdenago Baca and grandnephew of Elfego Baca, Rio Rancho, New Mexico.

The early 1880s brought two major events to Socorro: the train and the newspaper. The train was the Atchison, Topeka and Santa Fe Railway, and the newspaper, the *Socorro Sun,* started in 1880 by A.M. Conklin. Eight wholesale and retail saloons advertised in the first edition of the *Socorro Sun* newspaper. With the influx of miners, cowboys, and immigrants, the number of saloons increased dramatically. By the mid 1880s, the A T & SF rail line was shipping goods from the east and bringing immigrants to the tiny village.

Socorro was now on-the-map and things were loud, rowdy, and busy. The plaza, where Elfego's Uncle Juan Jose Baca's mercantile store stood was surrounded by saloons: The Oasis, The Little Gem, The Smelter and Sample Room, Armstrong's White Elephant, and Our

Office. Baca's store also sold whiskey and wine by the glass at the counter.

In addition, several large hotels nearby sold drinks and advertised live entertainment. The Spanish Franciscans had been growing and making wine in the region for years. Even before the railroad, New Mexico was the fifth largest producer of wine in the country. Local wine would have been a popular drink in the 1880s. With the new railroad making ice more readily availability, cold beer grew in favor at the local saloons.

Grand Hotel, Socorro, New Mexico, circa 1880s. Photograph reproduction courtesy of the Socorro Historical Society.

Working along the plaza must have been exciting for young Elfego, exciting and scary at times. The majority of the new arrivals were Texas cowboys and eastern miners, who by nature didn't think much of *Mexicanos*. The Texas cowboys enjoyed 'treeing' Socorro with gunfire and bar fights, and shootings were frequent. The miners from Magdalena would stay in town on Saturday night and often brawl with the cowboys.

At the time Elfego worked at the mercantile, Pedro Simpson was elected Socorro County Sheriff. Simpson was an educated man and was of Anglo and Hispanic heritage; he was a man who appealed to the masses and was easily elected.

Keeping the peace in Socorro was no small job for Sheriff Simpson which included dealing with the cowboys. Their disregard for life and property was common place. According to the cowboys, 'treeing' was considered harmless fun, but to the townspeople it was frightening and usually costly. Dogs, animals, buildings, and sometimes people were considered fair game. The cowboys usually were in groups and often liquored-up, creating a problem for any single lawman or citizen to take action against them. It was a common occurrence in towns throughout the western frontier, considered 'normal' to the cowhands and accepted by most of the citizens, who could not defend against it.

While 'treeing a town' is not common terminology in the 21st century, many western movies, such as *Tombstone* (1993), *Forty Guns* (1957) and *Lawman* (1971), just to name a few, depict this type of behavior.

Although not addressed in his autobiographies, Elfego's first direct involvement in law enforcement in Socorro came in 1883 when several cowboys were 'treeing' the county seat. Sheriff Simpson pursued them out of town north toward Escondida. Many years later, Elfego informed Janet Smith, a Works Projects Administration interviewer, that he joined this chase:

> I had gone to Escondida a little way from Socorro to visit my uncle. A couple of Texas cowboys had been shooting up the town of Socorro. They hadn't hurt anybody that time. Only frightened some girls. That's the way they did in those days — ride through town

> shooting at dogs and cats and if somebody happened to get in the way — powie! — too bad for him. The Sheriff came to Escondida after them. By that time they were making a couple of Mexicans dance [in Escondido], shooting up the ground around their feet. The Sheriff said to me, "Baca, if you want to help, come along, but there's going to be shooting."
>
> "We rode after them," added Baca, "and I shot one of them [from] about three hundred yards away. The other got away — too many cottonwood trees in the way"[72]

The Santa Fe *Daily New Mexican* reported the story as a 'tragic event' and reported the victim was a Texas cowboy in his early twenties named Townsend, from Brownwood, Texas. Another Texan was wounded, but got away.

A Texas cattleman, a former Englishman named Frank Collinson, who was in Socorro at the time of the incident, called the shooting senseless, complaining that Sheriff Simpson and the deputy did not attempt to arrest the cowboy, but simply chased him down, shooting and killing him:

> "There was no harm in any of them," Collinson complained . . . "It was a wanton killing," Collinson finally charged.[73]

Collinson's complaints were obviously pro-Texan. His statement "there was no harm in any of them," when referring to the cowboys is incredible. The Texans were out-of-control and often against the Hispanic population. Obviously, Collinson viewed the behavior as normal.

One would conclude Sheriff Pedro Simpson deputized young Elfego for the above incident. Deputies were often sworn in on horseback, with or without a badge. Collinson referred to Elfego as an unnamed deputy. One would also conclude that his deputy status was legal, as no charges were brought against him for the shooting of Townsend.

The locally elected sheriffs had little help from the U.S. Marshals, especially to control local affairs. The New Mexico Marshal from 1876 to 1882 was John E. Sherman Jr. Marshal Sherman was tested mightily over his tenure. Much of New Mexico was wild and uninhabited. The Colfax County War and then the Lincoln County War dragged on through most of the 1870s. Outlaws, whiskey runners, rustlers, range wars, and general unrest pulled the Marshal's staff in all directions:

> "A virtual reign of terror" gripped the territory in 1876, and respectable citizens were "paralyzed" in "fear of their lives." The new Chief Justice Henry L. Waldo concluded that the vital organs of justice were diseased.[74]

Many of Sherman's problems trying to provide marshals and law enforcement in the territory were due to problems outside of his control. The lawmen coped with legislative mismanagement and lack of funding, while sheer time and distance stopped effective control of the numerous outbreaks of lawlessness. Every region of his district experienced serious violence.

Socorro was one of the original counties created by the Territorial Legislature Act of 1852. It was the largest county in the territory, with an area of 15,386 square miles. The county extended from central New Mexico across to the Arizona Territory. The county had thousands of square miles of rough and rugged terrain. It was home to Apache, Navajo, Zuni, Acoma, and other tribes still roaming this vast county. Outlaws had hideouts around every turn. Finding a man or cow in this mountainous and desolate part of New Mexico was a monumental job.

A local sheriff, such as Pedro Simpson in Socorro, was basically on his own to manage this huge territory. He was described as a good man, possessing fluency in both English and Spanish; however, he must have been completely outgunned.

The Texas cattleman's influx into Socorro County also targeted Socorro County politics. The newly arrived cattlemen wanted to oust Sheriff Pedro Simpson and other officeholders, and elections were looming in November of 1884. Sentiments were already running high against Sheriff Simpson because he failed to protect a Texas prisoner, Joel Fowler, from the vigilantes in Socorro. Joel Fowler was a reportedly wild and murderous type who unleashed his vengeance when drunk. But, he was a Texan! Not only had Sheriff Simpson failed to protect Fowler from the Socorro vigilantes, he had reportedly killed another Texan earlier that year in a questionable confrontation. Simpson had political enemies and they were the Texas cattlemen.

One day while Elfego was working at his uncle's store, about the middle of October in 1884, Deputy Pedro Sarracino came to the mercantile store to visit his brother-in-law and Socorro Mayor, Juan Jose Baca, who was the owner of the store.

Elfego said Sarracino lived in the San Francisco valley, on the extreme western part of Socorro County and he was the Deputy Sheriff at Frisco Plaza. The San Francisco valley was about one hundred and twenty miles west of Socorro.

Elfego described Sarracino coming to the store in Socorro and relating the problems in Frisco in his autobiography:

> About the middle of October, 1884, a man by the name of Pedro Saracino [Sarracino], brother-in-law of Jose Baca owner of the store where I was working. He had a big Deputy's badge. He came to talk to me frequently at that time and told me that while he was Deputy Sheriff at Lower Frisco, because the cowboys at the time were raising all kinds of disturbances. He told me that if he arrested anybody that his life would become thereafter in danger.
>
> He told me that before he left Frisco for Socorro about six or seven cowboys, drinking at his place got a hold of a Mexican called "El Burro". They laid him on the counter, one of the boys sat on his chest and arms and another one on his lap and right there and then the poor Burro was alterated [castrated] in the presence of everybody.
>
> Then a man by the name of Epitacio Martinez happened to be present,

objected and begged them not to do that. The result was that after they finished with Burro, the same cowboys got hold of Epitacio Martinez and measured about twenty or thirty steps from where they were and tied him. Then they used Epitacio as a target and betted the drinks on who was the better shooter. Martinez was shot four different times. But still he didn't die, he finally died in Gallup about two years ago, he also had a brother by the name of Tomas Martinez who is still living.

I told Saracino [Sarracino] the deputy sheriff that he should be ashamed of himself, having the law on his side to permit the cowboys to do what they did. He told me that if I wanted to, I could take his job. I told him that if he would take me back to Frisco with him, that I would make myself a self-made deputy. We left for Frisco about two or three days after that on a buck-board with a big mule. Half of the time we had to help the mule climb every steep hill. When in Frisco he took me to his house. I was expecting to run up against anything any minute.[75]

The Hispanics in the San Francisco valley were living in constant fear from the Texas cowboys having their way over the three hamlets: Upper Frisco, Middle Frisco, and Lower Frisco Plazas. Law enforcement in the

Frisco valley consisted of Justice of the Peace Lopez and Sheriff Simpson's Deputy, Pedro Sarracino.

The small population of the Frisco valley was primarily of Spanish descent. Most were farmers or sheepherders. In the early 1880s, the large cattle ranches had come to the lush valley, ranches such as the large John B. Slaughter Ranch with an estimated 150 ranch hands.

Milligan's liquor emporium was the local hangout, especially on Saturday night. Gunfights and rowdy behavior was common.

The local population had serious doubts that the local law enforcement had either the numbers or spine to keep the peace, leaving them basically unprotected by the law. Socorro County was a large area of land and the sheriff was in Socorro, over a hundred miles away. The only true law was the six-shooter. The crescendo to a huge confrontation between the Hispanic villagers and the newly arrived Texas cattlemen was growing daily.

The Hispanic villagers were horrified after the Texas cowboys castrated a man nicknamed *el Burro* and took target practice on Epitacio Martinez when he tried to stop them. Epitacio Martinez was shot four times, but lived. In another incident it was reported some Texas cowboys lassoed a *señorita,* dragged her off, and nobody knew what happened to her afterward.

The Hispanic population of Frisco needed a savior, a miracle. Elfego Baca stood up.

Deputy Elfego Baca Arrives

Why did nineteen-year-old Elfego volunteer to go to the San Francisco valley to defend the Hispanic villagers? Where does this kind of bravery come from, when he knew the odds would be against him? Was it in the spirit of his Spanish ancestors that he drop his apron, grab his guns, and ready himself to go to war? Marc Simmons wrote about Cristóbal de Oñate going to war against Indians when he helped conquer Nueva Galicia, which could be applied to Elfego:

> His military experience was nonexistent. Still, he was the beneficiary of the long Spanish tradition of militarism that grew from centuries of conflict with the Moors. Noble, merchant, artisan, peasant, and even clergyman had learned to provide for his own defense. Every man in his home and fields became a warrior. To leave one's shop or lay down one's plow on short notice and go soldiering became as natural to a Spaniard as breathing.[76]

Elfego's life had been personally affected by the conflicts between Anglos and Hispanics, especially since his return to Socorro. For the last three years he lived in Socorro during the reign of Eaton's vigilantes, and no doubt had felt fear and indignation from his treatment as a Spanish-heritage resident. Although the Baca name had been well-respected, it is not known whether there was any negative sentiment against the Bacas after the incidents of 1880:

> The hanging of his brother Onofre by the vigilantes in Socorro, also, hung heavy on his heart. After the hanging, the Spanish in Socorro lived under the threat of the vigilantes for three years. Elfego was ready to go to war with Texans when he volunteered to go help the settlers in the San Francisco Valley.[77]

There is a controversy in the stories over why Elfego went to Frisco. Several accounts say he went on a political campaign. Elfego disputed it in a New Mexico Works Projects Administration interview with Janet Smith later in his life:

> "Hell, I wasn't electioneering," he said gruffly, "I don't know where they got that idea. I couldn't have made a speech to save my life."

It is highly doubtful he was campaigning at nineteen. He was a store clerk in Socorro and would not embark on any political career until much later. The only political overtones of his trip were on behalf of Sheriff Simpson, who needed to send help to the residents of the San Francisco valley.

With his deputy badge in hand, Baca hopped onto Pedro Sarracino's mule-drawn buckboard, and the two men made the several day, 120 mile trip, to San Francisco Plaza. Most accounts assume Sarracino and Elfego arrived late on October 27 or early the next day.

Gravestone of Pedro Sarracino, located in the Saint Francis Cemetery, Middle Frisco Plaza. It reads, Pedro C. Sarracino, born 1850, died 1902. Photograph taken by the author, 2012.

The Hispanics of the San Francisco valley were not impressed when they saw the young deputy accompanying Deputy Sheriff Sarracino on his return from Socorro. They wondered why he had brought such a green horn to protect them from the Texans:

> One day a young deputy sheriff named Elfego Baca rode over from Socorro. He said that he was looking for a certain Texas cowboy who had been causing trouble with his drinking and shooting. Such duties were rather new to Elfego Baca, who had studied to be a lawyer.
> When Uncle Espedion Armijo first saw the smooth face and guileless eyes of Elfego, he bristled. He muttered to his

relatives that the people in Socorro must think little of the inhabitants of Reserve [San Francisco Plaza], for they sent a boy to defend them from a herd of barbarians! How could anyone as young-looking as Baca win respect as a sheriff?

One bright warm day a number of Spanish people met at a farm to thrash wheat. A large dinner was in preparation at the farm home, and Elfego joined the crowd of guests. Just before the dinner, Uncle Espedion Armijo and some of the men had a private meeting inside the house — probably to discuss their plight. Sheriff Baca was left outside with young Petrocinio [Patrocinio, younger brother of Epitacio Martinez] and other boys, who were playing games. Suddenly Elfego asked one of the boys to toss a can in the air. As the object descended, Elfego's gun materialized in his hand and five shots stabbed through the can.

The men, glancing out the window, saw Baca casually inspecting his riddled target. Uncle Espedion was visible affected by the sight, declaring there might be some use for Baca after all.[78]

It is believed by most sources that the date was October 28, 1884, when the first encounter with the Texas cowboys began.

Elfego was talking to Justice of the Peace Lopez, when a couple of cowboys wildly rode in shooting up the Upper Frisco Plaza, before going into Milligan's for more liquor. Elfego asked Justice Lopez why that behavior by the cowboys was allowed. Lopez told him it couldn't be stopped, because the Slaughter Outfit had around 150 cowboys, and if they did, the Slaughter bunch would cause the village a lot of harm. He told Elfego when they came to town in bunches; they shot dogs, chickens, cats, and anything else that moved.

Elfego was disgusted with the backbone of the law in Frisco. Pedro Sarracino and the people of the village were afraid of retaliation from the gun-toting Texans:

> . . . it was especially at the mercy of the hired employes [sic] of one Slaughter, who yearly drove his herds through from Texas to Western Socorro, picking up what stray native cattle happened to be in the way and finally arriving at his ranch near Frisco with considerable wealth.
> There had been remonstrance about this, but no action, for the Slaughter outfit was well heeled and a bit rough and quick on the trigger. There was even less remonstrance among the terror stricken inhabitants of Frisco. Should the Justice of Peace seek so far to retain his legal dignity as to incarcerate one of the offenders, it would be simply an excuse for the jolly Slaughter boys to come down and practice target shooting at his fleeing form and to kick open the jail and take out their little pal. The Slaughter outfit, in short, was a law unto itself.[79]

Elfego told Justice Lopez, "that when such things were tolerated it only made the cowboys bolder, and that it should be stopped at once." He insisted they should not let the Americans living among them get the impression that the Mexicans were afraid of them:

> "I will show the Texans there is at least one Mexican in the country who is not afraid of an American Cowboy," he told Justice Lopez.[80]

Author's Note: The Memorial plaque reads '. . . one Mexican in the county,' but several other sources use '. . . one Mexican in the country.' This author believes Elfego was only asserting himself in the county of Socorro and not the entire country.

It did not take long for trouble to start. While Elfego was talking to Justice Lopez, he saw a cowboy gun butt another cowboy on the head two or three times. The cowboy fired off five rounds before Elfego walked over to him, and told him to quit, telling the cowboy he was a deputy. The cowboy turned and shot Elfego's hat off of his head.

That incident started the war between Elfego Baca and eighty plus Texas cowboys. Elfego remanded the young cowboy, Charlie McCarty, for trial and McCarty paid his fine and was released. However, it was not long before more trouble erupted again:

> Securing a few drinks of liquor at a store kept by a man named Milligan, he had proceeded to shoot up the place. Riding back and forth in the street, he

shot at everything, animate and inanimate, which met his gaze.[81]

Elfego would later give an account of the incident in his testimony at his trial in May 1885:

". . . at 2 o'clock I was at Milligan's, and McCarthy, my [former] prisoner, commenced firing off his revolver, at everything and everybody; Milligan went out [of his store] yelling; he knew I was a deputy sheriff, and asked me to help him; when I asked McCarthy to stop . . . he fired the last of the five shots at me; then I went home and got some men to help me arrest him, because I had no arms at the time; I got eight or nine men and went back to Milligan's house and did not find McCarthy there."

Elfego refers to the cowboy as Charlie McCarthy, as do many other accounts, but the spelling of the cowboy's name is McCarty.

Elfego and his 'posse' arrived at Milligans to find McCarty gone. He learned the cowboy was a cowhand at the Slaughter ranch. Elfego and a man named Francisquito Naranjo, Elfego called him a very brave man, went to the Slaughter ranch to arrest McCarty. McCarty tried to escape out a backdoor avoiding arrest, but Elfego apprehended him and took him to Deputy Sheriff Sarracino's house located at Lower Frisco Plaza.[82]

The depictions of the incident can have strikingly different context depending upon the source. James H. Cook describes his version of the incident in his book *Fifty*

Years on the Old Frontier. James Cook recollected the events during the arrest of Charlie McCarty:

> Baca went out at once and arrested and disarmed McCarty with but little trouble; for he was really not a bad man — merely a little too playful at times.[83]

The account by James Cook explains how the behavior of drunken cowboys was not only tolerated by Texans, but dismissed as just playful. Shooting people and castrating men was not playful fun, at least not when you are on the receiving end of the playful spirit.

William French, in his book *Some Recollections of a Western Ranchman*, was a bit more honest in his writings on how the Texans felt about the Hispanic villagers in the San Francisco valley:

> He [Elfego Baca] had been staying in the plaza for some days when some of the cowboys from the neighboring ranches, having ridden in and sampled some of Mr. Milligan's forty-rod whiskey, recollected that they were citizens of the great State of Texas and that the Alamo and other historical events were closely connected with the despised Greaser. Under the influence of patriotism and whisky they proceeded to give vent to their feelings.[84]

In other words, 'Remember the Alamo' gave Texas cowboys license to harass Hispanic villagers, castrate *el Burro,* and shoot Epitacio Martinez when he tried to stop them from performing the heinous deed:

> Amongst those whose absence from Texas was tolerated only on the grounds of saving expense to the State were many cowboys who lost no opportunity of displaying their hatred of Mexicans. To them all Mexicans were 'Greasers' and unfit associates for the white man.⁸⁵

Elfego brought his prisoner to the Justice of the Peace. He refused to hear the case, fearing retaliation from the Slaughter cowhands. Elfego then decided he would take his prisoner to the County Seat in Socorro. Unable to start immediately for Socorro, Elfego took McCarty to a location in the Middle Plaza to a private residence.

By this time, the Slaughter cowboys were not going to let a 'greaser' Mexican take one of their own. They headed to Middle Plaza looking for Baca on the night of October 28, 1884. The Slaughter cowboys led by their foreman, Young Parham, confronted Baca and demanded the release of McCarty:

> That night twelve cowboys demanded the release of the man I had under arrest. They were armed to the teeth. I told them that instead of releasing the prisoner I was going to give them time enough to count from one to three before I shoot.⁸⁶

Elfego was outnumbered and the mob of twelve Slaughter cowboys were angry and well armed. It was a vigilante group looking for their kind of justice. Elfego, having lived in Socorro with the vigilantes, knew the probable outcome. He would not have been reluctant to use his weapons and shoot to protect himself and the prisoner, but gave the cowboys to the count of three to withdraw. The group of twelve Slaughter cowboys was led by the ranch foreman, Young Parham:

> **They undertook to draw their weapons, then I started "one, two, three" and fired. When I fired they ran, I killed one man and horse on the run. I hung on to my supposed prisoner.**[87]

Young Parham's horse was hit and fell on Parham. Another cowboy named Tabe Allen was shot on the knee by Elfego. Elfego held on to his prisoner. Parham lived through the night, but died the next day from being crushed by his horse.

The Slaughter cowboys gathered their wounded and retreated. Although it would seem the twelve cowboys could have stormed the house, they respected the grit, determination, and skills of young Elfego. They needed reinforcements!

Mexicans on the Warpath

According to his autobiography, Elfego's response to the Slaughter cowboys when they came to take McCarty stunned them more than Parham's death. The fact that a Mexican fired back at Texas cowboys was something they couldn't believe. The Slaughters sent riders out in all directions to round up all the Americans, telling them that the Mexicans were on the warpath wanting to kill Americans.

It was customary to consider only whites or Anglos, 'Americans,' when talking or writing at the time. Any Spanish-heritage persons, regardless of where they were born, were called 'Mexicans.' Most of the inhabitants of the Frisco valley were Hispanics who had been given American status via the Treaty of Guadalupe Hidalgo in 1848. Although New Mexico was not yet a state, it was a U.S. Territory in 1884 and all citizens had equal rights, well at least on paper they did. We see this type of writing in the following excerpts.

James H. Cook, in his book *Fifty Years on the Old Frontier,* wrote his recollection of what the rider said when he stopped at his ranch:

> One evening in the fall of 1884, a rider came at a furious gait up to my ranch house door and hurriedly informed me that the Mexicans had gone on the warpath at a little settlement up the San Francisco River, about thirty miles away. He stated that they had killed one of Mr. Slaughter's cowboys and were going to try to wipe out all the Americans living near their settlement. This Mexican

settlement was known as the San Francisco Plaza. It was divided into three sections, called the Upper, Middle, and Lower Plazas. The rider told me that he had been sent to warn Americans living along the San Francisco River of their danger and to get as many men as possible to go immediately and help guard the homes of the Americans living near the Mexican settlement.[88]

William French reported the same incident in his book *Some Recollections of a Western Ranchman:*

> Things were going along smoothly when one afternoon we were startled by a messenger from our friends at the S U [Slaughter Ranch]. This man brought word that there was trouble between the Mexicans and the white settlers. A cowboy from the Spur Ranch had been killed and the Mexicans were holding another in captivity at the plaza. It was feared an attack would be made on some of the outlying ranches, especially the S U, which was nearest to them. He had come for assistance and for an officer of the law. The only white deputy within reach was Dan Bechtol over at Alma. We told the messenger to go ahead to Alma and we would wait for his return. If the deputy brought a posse along we could all go to the S U together.[89]

James Cook and his WS ranch hands arrived at the Slaughter ranch around midnight and found cowboys and ranch hands from other ranches gathered there. They too had been asked to come to the San Francisco Plaza, because the Mexicans were on-the-warpath. Cook wrote:

> Before daylight 'quite a number of Americans' had collected at the Slaughter ranch. While they waited there at the Slaughter place, Cook wrote they sent two men, well known there in the settlement to find out what the Mexicans were doing. They returned, only to report one Mexican named Elfego Baca, arrested a Slaughter cowboy for disturbing the peace.[90]

William French wrote he and his cowhands arrived at the Slaughter Ranch around one o'clock in the morning, expecting to find the place in flames:

> According to the gentleman who had come to summon us, Mr. McCarthy was an inoffensive youth incapable of harming an insect. After his departure to Alma to procure legal authority, we started out on our own hook and reached the S U around one o'clock in the morning. Instead of finding the place in flames we found them all asleep. We roused them up, demanding to know where the enemy was, and they said he must be in bed. We had got in and settled down when Mr. Bechtol and the

> Alma contingent arrived, accompanied by the belated messenger. They were all full of zeal and whiskey, and the representative of the law, Dan, was especially ferocious; and although nobody was actually holding him, he expressed a determination that if he was only allowed to get at them not one would be left alive on the following day.[91]

James Cook and William French arrived at the Slaughter Ranch with their cowboys ready for a 'Mexican War.' All they found was one Deputy Sheriff Elfego Baca holding Charles McCarty on a charge of disturbing the peace. Both Cook and French were told by the Slaughter cowboys that Charlie McCarty was a harmless young cowboy, who wouldn't hurt a flea on a dog's back. They felt the Mexican deputy was way out of line in arresting him. McCarty was just having fun, doing what they always did when they rode into the settlement shooting it up.

The army of cowboys now at the Slaughter Ranch selected two men to go to where Elfego held the prisoner and attempt to negotiate for a quick trial and release:

> We held a council and decided to select one or two of our number to go to the Plaza, see the Justice of the Peace and Mr. Baca, and try to arrange for the trial of McCarty at the Plaza; for the charge against him was not a desperately serious one, and we all realized that considerable trouble might be started.[92]

Two men were sent to the Plaza to talk to Baca: Clemente Hightower and Gyrone Martin. Baca referred to one of the men as Gyrone Martin, although he may be Jerome Wadsworth. Elfego said the pair arrived on horseback at eight o'clock in the morning. Elfego knew Clemente Hightower by name. Clemente and Gyrone stood about two hundred yards away, demanding he take the prisoner to the Upper Plaza. Elfego pulled his two guns and played with them in their direction, and told them that he would, singlehandedly, deliver the prisoner for trial. They informed Elfego there were about one hundred cowboys in the valley waiting for him to go by there.[93]

Hearing the number of Texas cowboys in the valley, Elfego gathered the women and children and told them, if they didn't want to get killed or hurt, they must all go to the Catholic Church in the Middle Plaza. When Elfego left with his prisoner to Upper Plaza, he estimated about one hundred and twenty-five villagers were in the Saint Isidore Mission Church. Now, the Hispanic villagers were afraid the Texans were on the warpath.

One can only imagine how the villagers felt holed up in the church. One young deputy could not protect them from a mob of well-armed Texas cowboys. They themselves didn't have the arms to match the Texans. For all they knew, the Texans would kill Elfego and then come after them. James Cook admitted:

> The inhabitants of the three hamlets were alarmed and feared that the cowboys intended 'to clean out the Mexicans.' He learned 'all the Mexicans living within a day's ride' had been summoned.[94]

Between the call to arms to the neighboring cowboys and the summons sent to the Hispanic families of the area, it was quite likely the population of the Frisco valley had swelled to historic proportions. Fear and agitation was rampant on both sides.

When Elfego arrived at the Justice of the Peace at Upper Frisco Plaza, a large group of cowboys were waiting for him. He wasted no time and took the prisoner McCarty inside. Returning outside of the building, he greeted the crowd of cowboys:

"Good Morning, Gentlemen."

The exact number of cowboys assembled at this time ranges from the twenties to the eighties. The late-arriving cowboys, who accompanied Deputy Bechtol, had been up most of the night and likely slept late. Dan Bechtol seemed more interested in sleeping-off his late night activities.

The trial didn't last long. McCarty was fined $5, which he paid, and was released:

> When Baca came out he saw two cowboys he knew, one named Wilson, and greeted him, "Good morning, Mr. Wilson."
> "Hello, you little Mexican, etc. etc.," Wilson replied by cursing at him.[95] [Baca was kind enough not to repeat the derogatory remarks uttered by the Texas cowboy.]

Looking around Elfego saw an army of cowboys waiting outside the Justice of the Peace's house. All were armed and some were drunk. Someone in the crowd fired a shot behind or near Baca and everyone ducked. Elfego believed the shooter didn't fire directly at him, because there were many cowboys behind him, and the bullet could have hit one of the other cowboys.[96] With the plaza full of Texas cowboys, Elfego wasn't surprised by the gunshot.

Memories of mob rule in Socorro must have flooded his mind. The vigilante lynch mob had hung his brother, Onofre, and the odds were against him now. Quickly he drew his colts and backed away taking refuge in a mud shack called a *jacal*:

> I drew my guns and backed up to a picket house called [a] "Hackal" [jacal] belonging to a man by the name of Geronimo Armijo. Molo Armijo, his son who must have been about eight years old now living in Magdelena, was on the roof [of] the so-called "Hackal" husking corn. He and another boy went down in a hurry. I went into the house and put the lady and children out, then the fight started.[97]

"Vamos!" yelled Baca. "Get out before you're killed!"[98]

Believed to be a photo of the Armijo *jacal*, Upper Frisco Plaza, New Mexico.

Henry Martinez, great grandson of Epitacio Martinez holding a picture of the *jacal*. Behind is the Elfego Baca memorial. Henry pointed out the terrain in the background, which matches the background terrain in the picture. Henry wanted to locate the memorial as close to the actual site as possible. Photograph taken by the author, 2012.

The *jacal* belonging to Geronimo Armijo was a typical mud hut constructed with upright poles and plastered with mud on the inside and outside. The Elfego Baca monument sits on the documented location of Armijo's *jacal* in Reserve, New Mexico. While today the location is surrounded by buildings in the center of town, in 1884 the *jacal* would have been isolated and vulnerable.

Elfego would remain in the *jacal* for about thirty-six hours defending himself and keeping the cowboys at bay. They were not going to lynch or kill him without a fight.

Four-thousand Bullets

Now alone in the *jacal,* Elfego looked around at his surroundings seeing only simple furnishings. Wood coals were keeping the day's meal warm on the stove. He slowly walked around the mud hut peering out the small windows and cracks hoping to see what the Texas cowboys were doing. To say he was not scared would be a lie. Elfego was scared to death, the memory of his brother, Onofre, hung by vigilantes was imprinted in his memory. Outside he knew there was a gang of Texas cowboys, the same ones who had castrated *el Burro* and shot Epitacio Martinez. They were worse than the Socorro vigilantes and this time they were after him.

A loud cracking sound startled him and the door shuttered. Someone began kicking at it, and the door began to buckle. A gruff voice was yelling for him to come out. Elfego backed away and readied his colts.

The door cracked again from the outside. Elfego heard several voices yelling, "Come out you dirty greaser."

"Kick it again, Jim," a voice urged. "He's trapped like a rat."

A loud kick hammered the flimsy door again and Elfego fired his guns dead in the center of the door. A scream erupted from the other side:

> Close on Elfego's heels had come the Slaughter outfit, headed by Jim Herne, a Texan with a bounty over his head and a disdain for Mexicans in his heart. He got off his horse, dragged his rifle from its position on the saddle, and advanced toward the jacal inhabited by Baca.

"I'll get this dirty little Mexican out of here," he said. "Come on, you," he bellowed. "Come out of there, and come damned quick!"

Baca's answer was two revolver shots, both of which hit vital spots. Either of them was enough to kill Herne, and one did. Friends bore the body away hastily and the siege was on.[99]

William French wrote he was waylaid by Dan Milligan and James Cox, wanting him to have a drink before he left. They proceeded to Milligan's saloon and had the parting drink, where French said goodbye to his friends. McCarty was free and there was no reason to linger at the plaza. French said he was about to get on his horse and head to the S U [Slaughter] ranch where they would spend the night, before returning to their ranch in the morning. Hearne and several other cowboys came up to him and asked where Baca was. French recalled how Hearne was killed:

> I was getting him [his horse] loose when I was approached by the gentleman who had shot his gun off so close to my feet, accompanied by three others. They asked me if I had seen where Mr. Baca went when he came out of the court-room. I pointed out the cabin and was preparing to mount when they told me they had authority from the presiding justice to arrest Mr. Baca. The ostensible reason was the shooting of the man at the time of McCarthy's

arrest. They said it was only just that he should be made to answer according to law.

This sounded all right, so I said: 'Let's go ahead and arrest him.' The four of us walked down to the cabin. Hern, who had taken the lead, walked up to the door, and I followed close behind him. He knocked, asking if there was anyone there. Receiving no reply, he kicked the door violently, demanding admittance. The reply this time was decisive. It came in the form of a bullet through the door, which took him in the abdomen.

He swore a marvelous oath and fell back into my arms. I dragged him as quickly as I could around the corner of the cabin. The others scattered in all directions, but joined me almost immediately, and we laid him out on the ground.[100]

The battle was now under way. The first exchange of gunfire erupted after the shooting of Jim Hearne. The Texas cowboys began pounding bullets at the *jacal* hoping to kill the 'greaser.'

Bullets began hitting the shack from all directions. Elfego dropped to the sunken floor and could hear the lead whiz above him. Mud and splinters filled the air and covered his hat and shirt. A few hot lead balls fell on his pants legs. He wiped the sweat off his brow and thanked God the *jacal* had a sunken floor. It seemed like the shooting went on and on. After it stopped he cautiously rose up and carefully peeked through the cracks of the *jacal*. The door had dozens of bullet holes and the mud between the timbers showed daylight. Elfego peered out of a crack in the wall, careful to stay away from the window. He could see the cowboys hiding behind whatever cover they could find.

It was then that he noticed her; it was a statue of *La Nuestra Señora Santa Ana (*Our Lady of Saint Anne*)*, the mother of the Virgin Mary and grandmother of Jesus Christ. Saint Anne was the protector of the Virgin Mary. Elfego made the sign of the cross and prayed *la Señora* would protect him now.

Unknown to Elfego at the time, when Hearne and his friends approached the *jacal*, most of the cowboys were headed back to their respective ranches when the first shots were fired. As French recalled, he was saddling his horse getting ready to leave. James Cook recalled he was already on the trail when he heard the shots:

> We had proceeded but a short distance when we heard shooting back at the Plaza. Knowing that many Mexicans had gathered in the hills about the Plaza, we were afraid they might have attacked the remaining Americans there. We thereupon rode hastily back, scattering as we went. One of my men, my trusted friend Charlie Moore, rode with me. Upon reaching the Plaza we rode up rather close to one of the jacals, or Mexican huts. I could see no fighting going on; not a man was in sight. Moore started to swing down from his horse just as I saw smoke from a pistol shot floating from a window in the picket

house which we had approached. Calling to Charlie to look out, I spurred my horse and made a rather sudden start away from the front of that window. As I was about to reach the shelter of another building, a bullet tore off a bunch of adobe and filled my eyes with dust and dirt. The shot was fired from the adobe which we had first approached.

Riding around behind the Milligan store, I found a number of Americans. They were gathered about a man who was down on the ground, and whom I soon found to be dying. His name was Herne.

It appeared that, after McCarty was liberated, a few men, including Herne, had started out to find Baca. Baca had doubtless figured something of the sort would happen, for he had barricaded himself into a picket house, which made a very good fort. After searching for Baca in other parts of the Plaza, the crowd went to this picket house. Finding the door barred, they started to force it open. A bullet was fired through it from the inside. It struck Herne, but it also revealed the hiding place of Baca. Excitement now ran high. Baca must be killed or captured.[101]

Hearne was mortally wounded, but still conscious:

> His main anxiety was a desire to get even with the man who had shot him, so we promised that we would do all in our power to capture him and deliver him to the authorities.[102]

Now with Hearne dead or dying, the cowboys were more than determined to get that 'dirty stinking greaser.' They left Hearne's body behind Milligans after they promised to avenge him.

Looking for help, they sought out Dan Bechtol, the deputy sheriff from Alma and found him in the back storeroom of Milligans. He was resting and said he was exhausted and offered no aid to either side.[103]

Out on the Plaza, the cowboys positioned themselves behind any cover and began furious volleys of rifle and gunshots at the picket house.

Elfego heard shouts from across the dirt yard. They were yelling that Hearne was dead and it was time to kill the 'greaser.' They wanted him dead. He could see little out of the narrow cracks in the walls and was afraid to pop his head above the small window sill to get a better look. For the moment the shooting had ceased. He sank down into the sunken floor and assessed his situation. He knew there were lots of them and only one of him. Unbuckling his belt, he counted his extra bullets. There were about thirty-three and five more in each of his colts. It was not enough and he would have to use them sparingly. By the door sat an old rifle. Hopefully it had a few more cartridges.

Elfego sank further down into the sunken floor as more bullets whizzed overhead striking all around him. The Texans peppered the house with another volley. If they continued shooting at intervals riddling the *jacal*, rather than isolated shots, he might have time to keep them off guard. After the next volley, Elfego jumped up and looked for cowboys to come out from behind the short adobe walls and took a couple pot shots at them, only to see them scramble back for cover. He saw them trying to lure his fire, by one of them popping his head up, before another would fire at the window or door.[104] The walls had more peep-holes in the mud where the bullets had taken their toll. Elfego peered out of the back window and saw some people up on the far hill. They were too far away to be cowboys. There was no cover behind the *jacal*, so all of the cowboys seemed to be between him and the yard leading toward town and Milligans.

Elfego heard the cowboys yell out to him in Spanish, saying they wanted to talk with him. Elfego wondered why they were talking in Spanish, when they knew he spoke perfect English. By this time more cowboys heard the shooting, returned to the Plaza and reinforced their ranks:

> The day dragged slowly for young Elfego. In the jacal he found a plaster-paris reproduction of a saint, known as Mi Senora Santa Ana. Upon the head of the worthy saint, young Baca was wont to rest his Stetson hat in such a position as to be evident through the tiny windows of the hut to the impatient Texans. His own position would be in another part of the fort. Attempts to take Baca by surprise were met by well aimed shots that discouraged them. To make things more difficult for the imprisoned young man, the cowboys stretched blankets between houses

> where they were located. It gave Baca nothing to fire at, and it gave the Slaughter troupe a splendid vantage point for attack.[105]

Elfego timed the cowboy's volleys, returning shots sparingly. He didn't want to waste his limited supply of bullets. He could see the cowboys had stretched blankets between the buildings and walls to conceal their positions and movements. After the last volley ended, he moved the statue of Saint Anne to the opposite side of the *jacal*, re-perching his hat on her head so it was visible from the window. He noticed she had not been hit yet. Suddenly bullets started flying into the window and the cowboys began another siege. Elfego hit the deck watching and feeling the bullets zing by overhead. This cat and mouse game went on for some time as the hours dragged on for both sides. At the end of the most recent volley, Elfego quietly crouched in the corner peering out of a crack:

> After a strong volley stopped and we were sure Baca must be dead, one of our ranks boldly walking up to see if he was killed. Elfego sent him back to cover with a volley of his own. William French identified the cowboy as Ed Erway.[106]

Shocked Elfego was still alive, the cowboys began another fierce volley on the *jacal*. Elfego retreated below floor level again thanking *la Señora* for the sunken floor.

William French recalled the look on the faces of the cowboys, when they realized Elfego was still alive:

> . . . we resumed our onslaught on the cabin, searching every nook and cranny

where a bullet could possibly penetrate. This had the effect of quietening [sic] him, for his demonstrations ceased; but where he sought shelter from our fire, and how he escaped the numerous bullets that must have passed through the building, was a mystery to us.[107]

Elfego lost track of time and realized he was hungry. The wood stove was still warm and he added a few logs. He found some beef and made beef-stew, coffee, and tortillas.[108] The cowboys seemed to be taking a break, too, as things quieted down. While he ate, he kept a keen eye on the movements of the cowboys. Now he had many bullet holes to look through and it amused him that he could see his enemy and they could not see him. He laughed when a cowboy attempted to rush the shack only to be driven back by a well placed shot at his feet. He could have easily killed the brave man, but only wished to scare him.

With night approaching, the cowboys were stumped as to how to dislodge their prey:

> Excitement now ran high. Baca must be killed or captured. Just how either was to be effected was a question. Many plans were suggested. By this time everyone was convinced that Baca would sell his life as dearly as possible. He was at bay and thoroughly aroused. One part was dispatched to the Cooney mining camp after dynamite with which to blow up the house in which he was barricaded.[109]

Long shadows covered the entire valley and night was on its way. The cowboys slacked off from their shooting and they posted guards to prevent Elfego from escaping during the night. Elfego recalled to his autobiographer, Crichton, how the cowboys threw dynamite at the *jacal*:

> Near midnight of the first night, Baca from his place of hiding saw a tiny light creeping along the ground in his direction. He was not aware of it — having at the time no knowledge of mining such as he was later to have — but what was approaching him was a lighted fuse attached to a stick of dynamite which had been secured from the Cooney mining comp [sic] by sundry of Slaughter's cowboys who galloped off in that direction when it was evident that young Elfego was not to be dislodged from his refuge without the demise of many.
>
> "I saw the light," relates Mr. Baca, forty years later, "but thought it was a cigarette butt thrown by one of the cowboys and being blown in my direction by the wind. I watched it curiously. It would be still for a moment and then it would come on again. I thought it was funny that a cigarette should keep lit that long, but I didn't know any other explanation of it. I didn't know what dynamite or a fuse was at

that time. The light kept coming and I kept watching and the next thing I know: BLOOEY!!!!"[110]

Elfego fell back against the rear wall, covered with dust from the blast. His hearing was impaired and his eyes itched from the dust. Shock kept him momentarily paralyzed, until he forced himself up and cleaned his eyes and face. By all reason he should be dead after the concerted effort by the cowboy's tremendous amount of bullets hitting the flimsy mud shack, and dynamite collapsing part of the structure. Perhaps, *la Señora Santa Ana* summoned Santiago, patron War Saint of the Spanish, the bearded, sword-wielding knight astride a white stallion and a band of angels, to protect him.

In the darkness he could see the collapsed wall had imploded in such a way there was rubble closing off the corner and it had not left a gaping hole exposing him nor giving him escape. He peered from the front corner of the *jacal* into the darkness expecting a charge of cowboys to rush him. Nothing seemed to be moving in the night. He kept his vigil for some time, before finally slumping in exhaustion. Apparently, the cowboys were afraid to attack:

> The cowboys didn't have the nerve to investigate the result of dynamiting the jacal, afraid Baca was still alive and would kill anyone who got near the shack. They waited for daylight, before anyone volunteered to approach the jacal. The cowboys were taken back when they spotted smoke coming out of the chimney. Elfego was still alive and cooking breakfast.

> And the fervent Texas curses threatened to dry up the Frisco with their vehemence. There was simply no dealing with a fellow as lucky as that! They took out their wrath in successive and vindictive volleys that hit every last remaining individual thing in the jacal except the form of one Baca.[111]

Twenty-six hours had gone by and Elfego was eating his breakfast when the next onslaught of bullets began. It was the morning of October 31, 1884. Elfego took his breakfast and sank to the floor as bullets whizzed above him. He had no idea how this was going to end, perhaps he would die at the hands of the Texas cowboys. He counted his remaining bullets, knowing he would use them all before the cowboys killed him. Likewise, the cowboys were not giving up. They were determined to get the 'greaser.'

It is interesting that throughout the recollections of Elfego, Cook, and French, the only Anglo lawman, Deputy Dan Bechtol, was missing-in-action. Deputy Bechtol was accounted as sleeping in the back room at Milligans. He was obviously not concerned with the battle raging across the street from where he slept.

Elfego finished his breakfast while waiting for the latest barrage to stop, then crept to his lookout position near the front corner:

> About ten o'clock, Baca saw a form start across the open space between the blankets of the Slaughter outfit and the hut wherein he stood. It was a cowboy sheltered behind the cast-iron front of what had once been a stove. He kept

well covered and he approached slowly and with care. Nothing showed above the cast-iron surface. The figure had all the appearance of a knight of old accoutered [sic] for the joust but minus the horse. The armour was home-made but highly effective. Elfego wasted no shots. He watched with a hawk-like eye for the first slip-up of the armoured Texan. He watched for the first mistake in the slow business-like crawl; he watched for the first errored appearance of the cowboy's head over the top of the rejuvenated stove. With patience his chance came. There was a fleeting second when the cowboy's discretion was not equal to his valor. He ventured a peek at his goal. It was his last peek of the day. The bullet from Elfego's gun entered his scalp and journeyed across the top of his pate and skimmed off into space.[112]

Elfego watched as the armoured knight dropped his shield to the ground and ran yelling back to the blankets. The cowboy ran back for cover wide-eyed, with blood pouring down his face. No other cowboy braved any more tricks, fearing Elfego's dead-eyed shooting.

Over the day, larger numbers of Hispanic villagers from the surrounding farms had converged upon Frisco, staying mostly on the surrounding hills. So far they had not ventured into the town or threatened the Texans, even though Elfego was cornered. Recollections of eleven-year-old Patrocinio Martinez, brother of Epitacio Martinez, vividly described the fear of the villagers:

> The next hours were filled with vivid and terrible impressions for Patrocinio. The Spanish men were meeting and collecting guns in Uncle Espedion's house high on the hill. He would never forget their grim, etched faces or their low, furious words that exploded like bullets. Then there were the puffs of gunfire below and the noise of the shots.
>
> In the Armijo home a decision was made. Three of the most daring young men among the Spanish must slip along to the brush jacal and rescue Elfego. Francisco Martinez [brother of Epitacio] and two others would go.
>
> They slipped from the hill, zigzagging toward the jacal. But before they reached it, an Anglo rancher had arranged a truce. Elfego Baca would be escorted back to Socorro.
>
> Young Patrocinio remarked, "I saw, from that moment, that I was going to have to defend myself in order to live."[113]

Espedion Armijo and Francisco Martinez were uncle and brother of Epitacio Martinez, who had been shot trying to save *el Burro* from these same Texans. Based upon the dates, Epitacio probably was still recovering from his gunshot wounds at the hands of the Texas cowboys. One might wonder why the Hispanic villagers, surrounding the scene in the hillsides, did not readily help defend Elfego. These people were farmers and sheep-herders and not gunfighters. They already knew the fire power of the Texans. For Espedion Armijo, Francisco Martinez, and the unknown man, this might have been a suicide mission. Luckily, help came from Socorro.

The cowboys had stopped shooting after Elfego shot the armoured knight and by now he was totally exhausted, pondering what they would do next. Unknown to him, help had arrived from Socorro:

> This was not a very exciting game, and the sun was getting low and we were all getting grumpy and drowsy when there was an unexpected diversion. This was a buggy containing three men, which drove in rapidly from the direction of Socorro. From it stepped a tall American, who said he was a deputy sheriff, and he actually possessed a badge to prove it. He had come in response to a report furnished by a Mexican, who was along with him in the buggy.
> Our own deputy, Dan, who did not sport a badge, and if he owned one must have left it at home, had up to this time taken no active part in the proceedings. But now he was very much in evidence, reciting what he had not done to enforce respect for the law . . . Mr. Rose now took charge, and another attempt was made to communicate with Mr. Baca,

through the medium of the Mexican who had come in the buggy.[114]

Approximately thirty-six hours had passed since Elfego had taken refuge in the *jacal*. Although the day before he had fired at the door in defense, unknowingly killing Hearne, he had not deliberately shot to kill. Suddenly he heard a familiar voice:

"Are you alive? Come on out; you're well protected!"[115]

Baca was startled out of his wits, both by the nearness of the voice, and by the fact it was the voice of his friend, Naranjo.

It was Naranjo who had accompanied Elfego to the Slaughter Ranch, just days before, to arrest Charlie McCarty. When things had turned ugly in Frisco, Naranjo rode to Socorro for help from the authorities. Elfego recognized the voice as Naranjo and trusted him:

"Naranjo!" he yelled, "is it you?"

"Si," bellowed out Naranjo in return. "It's all right. Come on out!"[116]

Elfego exited the *jacal* by the side window with a six-gun in each hand, pointed at the three men while scanning the area beyond them. He trusted no one. In his mind he could see vigilantes hanging his brother Onofre. His fears were well founded as the cowboys were still set on vengeance. He would go down fighting; no one was going to hang Elfego Baca:

> I told deputy Ross [Rose], "I am your prisoner but I will not surrender my guns."[117]

He could hear the cowboys yelling for his head and wondered if he should have come out.

Cook wrote that the cowboys, who had their rifles trained on Baca, wanted to hang him at once, but that he [Cook] dissuaded them from their intentions:

> I told them that we were a mob in the eyes of the law; that Baca had done things for which he could not escape being hanged; and that the laws of the land, not a mob, should attend to his case.[118]

The Mexican War or the Frisco Shootout was over. When they rode off, some of the Texans remembered Elfego Baca's words spoken before the fracas began:

> "I will show the Texans there is at least one Mexican in the county who is not afraid of an American cowboy."

Peace returned to the communities of Upper, Middle, and Lower Frisco. There were no further reports of atrocities against Hispanics in western Socorro County.

The procession took about a day and a half to arrive in Socorro. Elfego insisted on how he would be transported back to the county seat. He would ride on the rear of the buckboard. Deputy Rose would ride in front with the driver, A. M. Loftiss, and a group of six Slaughter cowboys would ride ahead of the wagon. Elfego demanded the six cowboys ride at least thirty paces ahead of them and he would keep his Colts loaded and handy.[119] Elfego arrived in Socorro both a hero and a captive. He was locked up in the new Socorro County jail, near where he was born:

> At that time they were building a jail in Socorro and I was put in it while they were putting the roof on it.[120]

Socorro Courthouse [foreground] with smaller jail building behind courthouse, circa 1890s. Photograph reproduction courtesy of the Socorro Historical Society.

It was estimated at Baca's trial for murder, approximately four thousand rounds were fired at the *jacal*. A broom handle had eight bullet holes; the door to the hut had three hundred sixty-seven bullet holes. Elfego was hit zero times; *la Señora Santa Ana* was hit zero times. One can only reflect — this man, like his ancestors, who survived war, famine, Indian attacks, and the harsh conditions of three hundred years, was destined to survive.

Elfego's Lasting Mark on Frisco

Before and during the gunfight between eighty Slaughter cowboys and one Elfego Baca at San Francisco Plaza, there was no documented effort of John Bunyan Slaughter intervening, nor attempting to stop the incredible fiasco. It could be assumed John Slaughter concurred with his cowhands 'treeing' the innocent settlement in order to put terror in people's hearts or in their terms 'having fun,' and took no notice of their actions against Elfego. Not one reference was made in any account of the events of late October 1884 that John Slaughter took part in or subdued or managed his men. In fairness, it is not known if he was actually in the San Francisco valley at the time or elsewhere. Although, according to his life biography he was living at his New Mexico ranch at that time.

Likewise, Deputy Sheriff Dan Bechtol did nothing to quell the mob. The accounts of both James Cook and William French indicate Dan Bechtol was sleeping-it-off at Milligan's store. Certainly, Sheriff Dan Bechtol had the authority and probably the respect of the Texas cowboys to control the shootout. The Texans had called upon him, as the only 'white' law enforcement in the vicinity. His efforts to manage the situation involved a lot of whiskey and sleep. It was remembered that he wanted to go and kill all the 'greasers.'

Both Slaughter and Bechtol had the power to stop the events of the Frisco Shootout, but they did nothing to stop it. After all, these were only 'greaser' Mexicans.[121]

James Cook, from the WS ranch, provided a much more level head and played a pivotal part in finally ending the standoff after Deputy Rose arrived from Socorro. Cook dissuaded the cowboys from overwhelming Rose and

Elfego and helped to calm the cowboys from further hostilities.

Although a localized event, no accounts of the four day siege at Frisco Plaza can be found in newspapers from that time. However, in contrast, the events of the A.M. Conklin murder raised alarm in the Anglo community. In fact, military troops were called into Socorro after the murder of Conklin. Newspapers from surrounding states carried the news.

On December 28, 1880, the *Sacramento Daily Record-Union* ran an article titled "Trouble at Socorro":

> Santa Fe, December 28th. – A very serious disturbance exists to-day at Socorro, N.M. The authorities refused to arrest the murderer of Conklin, editor of the Socorro Sun, and the citizens, finding no recourse at law, have arrested and hold by force the Sheriff and four others, including the murderer of Conklin. A rescue of the prisoners is threatened, and bloodshed is imminent. A request has been made on the military commander of the district for troops, and although the soldiers cannot be used as a posse commitatus, yet a company has been ordered from Colorado, N. M., as a means of protection for public property and the property of the railroad company. Bodies of men are being armed at Albuquerque and other points in the vicinity, and will go to Socorro to-night. Grave results may be expected. All the women and

children have been moved out of town. Acting Governor Ritch is doing all in his power to preserve the peace and to secure proper action of the law.

[Second Dispatch] Santa Fe, December 28th. – All the Americans have moved out of Socorro, and unless the troops reach there to-night a bloody fight will occur. The Sheriff, being a friend of Boca [sic], who recently killed Conklin, editor of the Sun, refused to arrest him, whereupon citizens swore out warrants and put the Sheriff and murderer in jail. The greasers threaten to rescue them. The Americans and the Atchison, Topeka and Santa Fe officers called on General Hatch for protection. Hatch ordered fifty soldiers from Wingate and a company of the Thirteenth Infantry from the town of Colorado to go to Socorro to protect Government property.

According to this article from the Sacramento, California newspaper, General Hatch dispatched fifty soldiers plus a company from the Thirteenth to Socorro on December 28, 1880, to control the 'greasers.' Perhaps up to 150 soldiers were sent, and the article also indicates residents had been evacuated. This seems to be an excessive response to a single random killing, but A.M. Conklin was Anglo and the assumed assailants were Mexican. One statement is interesting:

> . . . soldiers cannot be used as posse commitatus, yet a company has been ordered from Colorado, N.M., as a means of protection for public property and the property of the railroad.

Military troops were not allowed to provide help to a posse. A posse was organized by local law enforcement, U.S. Marshals, and local citizens who would be quickly deputized. Although no property in Socorro had been damaged or threatened, using this threat by the 'greasers,' allowed the military to order the use of troops to quell the Mexicans.

The events in Socorro following the killing of Conklin were carried in numerous newspapers in other states. One could argue that A.M. Conklin was a newspaper man, thus known in the business. Therefore, newspapers were more likely to print the story. An obscure newspaper, *The Carbon Advocate*, Lehighton, Pennsylvania, on January 1, 1881, carried the following article under "Crimes and Casualties":

> Socorro, January 1. – At a festival in Socorro, New Mexico, on Christmas eve, a disturbance arose among some Mexicans, which was quelled by A. M. Conkling, editor of the Sun. Soon afterwards, while Conkling and his wife were leaving the church, two Mexicans seized him by the arms, while a third shot him dead. The assassians [sic] fled to a neighboring village, where they reported to be "guarded by two thousand Mexicans." A large possee [sic]

of Americans, well armed, will endeavor to capture the murderers.

Surely, there could not have been anxious readers in Lehighton, Pennsylvania, located about eighty miles north of Philadelphia, concerned about the killing of Conklin, misspelled in the article as Conkling. Note the large number of two thousand Mexicans in the article. Perhaps this brought fear into the hearts of the people of Philadelphia.

The Socorro vigilantes rallied hundreds of Anglos into action to impose their law and order on the citizens of Socorro after the A.M. Conklin murder. Without elections and without badges they took control of Socorro, and they became the 'self-appointed' law in Socorro with safety in their numbers. When the Texans were harassing the Hispanic villagers of Frisco and other towns, the Socorro vigilantes did nothing. It was not their problem.

The 'treeing' of towns, the random killing of Hispanic civilians, the castration of a 'greaser,' warranted no press nor garnered any help from the law. Frisco had no newspaper. They had word-of-mouth. They had Deputy Pedro Sarracino to try to keep the peace. The Slaughter cowboys were well-heeled, heavily armed, loose and ready to shoot, and in large numbers. The Hispanic villagers of the Frisco valley had no power; they were helpless to change the course of events.

In October 1884 Elfego made himself the 'self-appointed' law or requested Sheriff Simpson to become a deputy to go to Frisco. When he was under siege by eighty or more cowboys in Upper Frisco Plaza, no troops were called in; no dispatch for military assistance was made; no effort was made to protect the citizens or public property in Frisco. In short, no newspaper accounts about the events in Frisco raised any alarm.

Elfego did not go to Frisco campaigning. He did not go to protect land or property. He did not go because he had friends or relatives in Frisco. He had no vested interest in Frisco. He unselfishly went to help strangers in need, strangers bonded by DNA. These strangers were bonded by a Spanish heritage that ran deep in his blood, strangers who laughed when they saw this young man of nineteen, small in stature and clean shaven. He looked an unlikely hero.

Without the press, without the law, and without the military, the Frisco Shootout was the longest and largest single shootout of the old west. By many viewpoints, it is the greatest gunfight of the old west — won by a Hispanic man, won by a Hispanic hero to the people of Frisco. It deserves this legacy today. He deserves this legacy today.

Elfego Baca was born just fifteen years after New Mexico became a United States territory in 1850. By 1884 New Mexico had been under United States control for thirty-four years. The influx of Anglos into this new territory grew with the coming of the railroad and lucrative mining. The population of New Mexico in 1870 was mostly native born New Mexicans, or people of Spanish descent. By 1890, about one quarter of the population had been born outside of New Mexico, mostly Anglos, and by 1910 the number was about one half of the total population. Before 1870 the number of incoming Texans was in the hundreds, but the volume of Texans incoming into New Mexico between 1870 and 1910 jumped from barely one thousand to over thirty thousand:

> European migrants were generally move adaptive to their environs [New Mexico] than their Anglo American counterparts, who often sought to impose on native western communities

> Anglo Saxon values and codes of behavior. As Anglo Americans encroached from the east, they brought with them distinct notions of God, property, industry, and capital, as well as fixed ideas of race.[122]

Like many towns in New Mexico, such as its much larger county seat Socorro, Frisco Plaza was settled by Spanish-descent families who had been in New Mexico for many generations. Elfego's ancestors had been in New Mexico since the time it was owned by the Spanish crown. They came for the crown and for the faith, overrunning the pueblo Indians and imposing their Catholic faith and values on the natives. These Spanish families came to set down roots, raise families and became part of the land itself. Families, like Captain Cristóbal Baca, came in 1600 without frills and fanfare, and endured extreme hardships to settle this land.

The Texas cattle barons came to the San Francisco valley to evade paying taxes to the State of Texas and because of the tick quarantine. They came to find grass and water for their thousands of head of cattle. They came to fatten the cattle and then to move on to Wyoming to sell them for profit, a profit that did not help the people of Frisco, except for Milligan's liquor emporium. They came to use the land and did not want any resistance.

New arrival to Socorro, A. M. Conklin, in his editorials in the *Socorro Sun* imposed his eastern Anglo values on the Hispanic citizens of Socorro. Within several months of his arrival, he was attempting to affect the local elections. Did he even know much about the long history of the families who had settled this area with the sweat of their backs and blood of their families? Doubtful. He wanted change; he wanted a change to an Anglo philosophy. After his death, the vigilantes took over and imposed those same values by force.

It is said, "To the victor goes the spoils." The architecture of the conquering Moors can be seen today in Spain. Only remnants of the great Aztec civilization are visible in Mexico's ancient temples. The Acoma's Sky City is one of the few pueblo locations remaining intact after the Spanish arrived in New Mexico. James Polk's Democratic platform of 'manifest destiny' pushed across the continent to conquer the Mexican government in the western territories. Americans were the conquerors and they felt the right to convert the new territory to their values.

The San Francisco valley was changed forever after Elfego's battle with the Texas cowboys in October 1884. John Slaughter maintained his ranch near Frisco until 1886, when a notice from the *El Paso Journal* was reported in the *St. Johns Herald* on May 27, 1886. He had sold his ranch on the Tularosa to Upcher and Stevens for a staggering $130,000:

> El Paso Journal. – J. B. Slaughter, who sold his Socorro county ranch and cattle not long since to Upcher & Stevens for $130,000, was in El Paso a short time since, enroute to Colorado City to visis [sic] his family. Mr. Slaughter has just returned from a horse-back trip from Socorro, across northwestern New Mexico and up into Utah territory, going to within 150 miles of Salt Lake City. He was ranch hunting . . .

The sale of the Slaughter Ranch in Frisco made John Slaughter a huge amount of money in 1886. This was no small ranch. This was no small amount of money pocketed by John Slaughter for the use of the land and water of the peaceful San Francisco valley.

James Cook left the Frisco area shortly after the Frisco Shootout and William French documented little interest in the four day shootout:

> After our little flutter at the plaza, things on the ranch returned to normal.[123]

Other ranches remained in the valley, trailing their cattle to the Magdalena train depot for sale. Some remain in the area today. Some descendents of Epitacio Martinez and Charlie McCarty also remain in Reserve, New Mexico. The remnants of the Slaughter ranch along the Tularosa River have all but blown away. Milligan's liquor emporium has long been demolished, remodeled, or rebuilt into the buildings of the current town of Reserve. The Saint Isidore Mission still stands in Lower Frisco. Pedro Sarracino, Clemente Hightower, and Epitacio Martinez are buried in local cemeteries, along with many others. The peaceful San Francisco River still flows gently along the valley.

Memorial sculpture of Elfego Baca by James N. Muir located in Reserve, New Mexico. Photograph taken by the author, 2012.

One cannot see into a man's heart and soul on a clean-shaven face. Elfego came to Frisco to help the people of the Frisco valley protect their lives against the Texas cowboys. After he was carted away on November 1, 1884, the atrocities of the Texas cowboys stopped.

Elfego Tried for Murder

Deputy Sheriff Frank Rose turned Elfego over to Justice of the Peace W. E. Kelly on November 4, 1884, upon their arrival in Socorro. Elfego was jailed and held for the murder of William B. Hearne. William Hearne was also called Bert or Burt Hurn or Hern or Will Herne, as variations of phonetic spellings, which were often used at that time.

Elfego sat in jail for over five months until the trial was held near Albuquerque's Old Town Plaza in an old adobe courthouse. Why it took so long to convene a judge and jury is not known and Elfego never elaborated on his time in jail. However a major event happened that might have dramatically changed Elfego's life or death.

Twenty-year-old Elfego Baca. Picture taken around the time he was being tried for the murder of William Hearne. Photograph courtesy of the private collection of Gilbert Baca, Elfego Baca's grandnephew, Rio Rancho, New Mexico.

Less than sixty days after the cell door slammed on Elfego, on January 1, 1885, Sheriff Pedro Simpson left office. He was replaced by the candidate of the cattlemen, Charles T. Russell. The new sheriff was another resident of Socorro County who had turned his back on Texas to find his fortune in the New Mexico Territory. With the Texans in charge, the cattlemen and the young hotheads they employed were suppressing their anger, and the Hispanics, for a while, were slow to take any lip from them. Racial relationships were upside down, at least on the surface. At the center of the tilted universe of Socorro County was Elfego Baca. The prior tenuous state of balance between the Americans and Mexicans, as both factions called themselves, would never be the same.[124]

Elfego was not indicted by the Socorro County grand jury until March 1885, at which time Elfego's attorneys arranged a change of venue, and moved the trial to Albuquerque, in Bernalillo County. He was charged with the premeditated murder of William B. Hearne. McComas and Field were the prosecuting attorneys for the New Mexico Territory. Shaw, Hamilton, and Rodey of Albuquerque were Elfego's defense attorneys.

His brother Abdenago Baca signed and paid his bond and was known to have been a man of substantial means. How Elfego paid for his high-profile legal team is not known. Perhaps Abdenago paid his fees, or perhaps his lawyers like their counterparts today, wanted the publicity of a high-profile trial and donated much of their time, or perhaps the Hispanic community helped to fund his defense.

The trial started on May 7, 1885. The chosen jurors were all Hispanic, a huge advantage for Elfego. The *Albuquerque Evening Democrat* carried the trial proceedings. The opening statement for the defense was made by John Shaw:

> Albuquerque, May 7th. – Baca was sheriff at San Francisco, that he had arrested McCarthy [McCarty] for discharging his pistol in the city limits, his cowboy friends went to town in full force and threatened to kill the sheriff and wipe out the town, that Baca in order to keep from being killed went to another house, and that if he did shoot the man, it was perfectly justifiable.

One question which has often been asked, was whether Elfego was a 'self-appointed deputy' or appointed by Sheriff Simpson. It was argued he bought a dime-store badge and was not a legal deputy. It was not uncommon for citizens to aid the law in the 1880s. Deputies were enlisted to help the under-staffed law enforcement in the form of posses and deputies. Like Elfego, they received no money or salary for their efforts. Instead, they put their lives on the line for nothing.

A hand-written document from Sheriff Simpson was produced as Defense Exhibit A:

> [I, P.A. Simpson, Sheriff] of Socorro County by these presents [sic] appointed Elfego Baca deputy sheriff for and in Socorro county and hereby authorize him to act in such capacity from and after this 26th day of Oct, 1884.
> [Signed] P. A. Simpson
> Sh. Soc. Co.

During the three day trial, the *Albuquerque Evening Democrat* provided a running, but choppy account of the trial. Charles McCarty was the first prosecution witness; unfortunately his testimony was never recorded. The second prosecution witness was named as James Wadsworth, identified in earlier accounts as Gyrone Martin or Jerome Wadsworth. Wadsworth and Clemente Hightower went to Middle Frisco Plaza to free Charles McCarty and accompanied McCarty with Elfego to Upper Frisco Plaza for trial. Wadsworth testified:

> "McCarty was standing just outside the door, and remarked, look at the crowd of men [cattlemen] coming here." Wadsworth added voluntarily that "they were all armed."

To the Hispanic jurors and trial attendees, the testimony surrounding the actions of Charlie McCarty and the 'treeing' of Frisco would have been a familiar event, reenacted in most frontier towns. Images of drunken cowboys, riding and firing into anything and everything, just as Charlie McCarty had done the day Elfego arrested him, would have grated at the jurors.

All the witnesses who testified against Elfego were the same cowboys who had trapped him in the *jacal* at Upper Frisco Plaza. There were no Hispanic villagers from Frisco called on Elfego's behalf. The trial was another shootout, with the Texas cowboys taking shots at the Mexican kid, who had upset the balance of Texan domination in Frisco.

Baca later stated the most notable defense were physical exhibits which had been brought from Frisco. The broom handle with eight bullet holes and the *jacal* door, about half the size of a regular door today, was riddled with three hundred and sixty-seven holes and had been reduced to a sieve.

In the end, however, it was probably Elfego's limit in the use of force during the Frisco events that stuck with the jurors. With his expert marksmanship he could easily have killed or wounded many, however Baca's restraint proved he was anything but a predator whose aim was to kill.

Elfego was found not guilty on the charges of killing William B. Hearne. The outcome of the trial vindicated Elfego. He had won in Frisco and he won in the courts, but the cowmen were still offended and not done with Elfego Baca.

Life after Frisco

Elfego met Francisquita Pohmer while he was being tried for the murder of Hearne. Francisquita was sixteen years old and a student at Sister Blandina's School in Old Town. She was the daughter of Joseph and Dolores Chavez Pohmer, who lived in Albuquerque. Her father was not happy about Francisquita seeing the infamous Elfego Baca.

Elfego asked Francisquita to marry him, and she told him she would if he was acquitted of the murder charges against him. Her father, a native of Germany, owned a meat market in Old Town and did his best to stop the relationship. As usual, love prevailed and Francisquita and Elfego were married on August 13, 1885.[125]

Francisquita Pohmer Baca around 1910. Photogram reproduction courtesy of Zimmerman Library, Center for Southwest Research, Elfego Baca Collection, University of New Mexico.

Starting in the fall of 1885 Elfego was tried for the murder of William Young Parham, the Texas cowboy who died when his horse fell on him. Parham and his Slaughter cowboy friends confronted Elfego at Middle Frisco Plaza demanding the release of Charlie McCarty. Elfego gave them to the count of three, before he fired on them, hitting one on the knee and Parham's horse, who fell on the cowboy. Parham died from his injuries. After a second trial at the hands of the cattlemen, Elfego was again found not guilty in March of 1886.

Notoriety worked two ways in the 1880s, as it does today. Young Elfego was as much a hero as he was a target. He had friends and enemies, and it can be said that he did not shrink away from his notoriety. At anytime or just around the corner, there could be some jasper wanting to shoot down the famous and invincible Elfego Baca, and others considered him 'charmed.' At twenty years old Elfego embarked on a lifelong journey, usually on the side of the law and always on the side of the Hispanics.

The Bernalillo County sheriff, Santiago Baca [no relationship to Elfego], deputized Elfego shortly after the trial. Elfego maintained his deputy badge for Bernalillo County until 1888.[126]

After Elfego Baca was tried twice for murder in connection to the Frisco Shootout and found not guilty, he and his new wife, Francisquita, lived in Albuquerque, later moving back to Socorro, or they may have kept a home and office in both cities. They had six children.

Elfego Baca as a young man in Socorro approximately twenty-five years old. Photograph courtesy of the private collection of Gilbert Baca, Elfego Baca's grandnephew, Rio Rancho, New Mexico.

Elfego became active in the community in law and politics of the day. In Socorro, his older brother Abdenago was active in the city and local politics, along with his uncle Juan Jose Baca, who was mayor. His brother's and uncle's position in the county may have helped pave the way for Elfego to follow a life in politics.

Abdenago continued in politics in the Socorro area, raising a family and serving sixteen years as the Socorro County Assessor. The A.B. Baca home, built in 1913, still stands on the corner near the plaza in Old Town Socorro. The Governor of New Mexico appointed Abdenago to the position of Socorro County Assessor in 1905, a position he held for sixteen years.

Abdenago Baca approximately fifty years old. Photograph reproduction courtesy of the private collection of Judge Robert T. Baca, grandson of Abdenago and Elfego Baca's grandnephew, Bakersfield, California.

In 1893 Elfego, following in Abdenago's footsteps, was appointed Deputy County Clerk of Socorro County and served through 1897. At that time, the position of county clerk was not paid by salary. He received compensation through fees charged for his services.

Elfego later said that while he was the county clerk, he refused to charge any fees in December and January of each year, in order to permit the 'poor people' of his county to obtain his services free of charge.

Elfego's life after Frisco has been well documented in detail by his other biographers. For most of his life he continued to serve the people of Socorro County in public service. He may have won some elections and lost some elections, won some trials and lost some trials, spending most of his life serving the public in New Mexico in some manner.

After studying the law in Socorro, he was practicing law as early as 1892. He was admitted to the New Mexico Bar in 1895 and in 1896 he was elected mayor of the City of Socorro and served through 1898. The memorial plaque of mayors, including Juan Jose Baca and Elfego Baca stands in Heritage Square, Socorro.

While he was mayor, the town of Socorro was threatened by smallpox and Elfego Baca made a bold move to protect his town:

> . . . a smallpox epidemic swept across New Mexico. Many died in Belen, then Sabinal, then La Joya. To the south San Marcial and San Antonio began reporting nearly daily deaths. This was an epidemic nobody knew how to deal with.
>
> Mayor Baca quickly decided to quarantine the entire town of Socorro. He placed armed guards on El Camino Real, the only road leading into and out of the city. Deputized armed men met each arriving train to prevent anyone from disembarking at Socorro. Ticket agents were given harsh instructions that only one way tickets could be sold. Whether you left by road or rail, you couldn't return.
>
> Elfego Baca completely isolated Socorro from the rest of the world. This was met with bitter opposition by some, but Baca's "hired guns" prevailed.

> However, no local cases of smallpox are reported in the Socorro Chieftain. Along the Rio Grande Socorro was the only sizable community to escape the wrath of the deadly 1897 – 1898 smallpox epidemic.[127]

In 1900 he served as School Superintendent of Socorro County for one year. While superintendent, he created his own 'stay in school' program out of his own pocket:

> In each district a $5.00 doll was given to the girl who had perfect attendance for the year, a medal to the boy. The system did a lot of good to the children in their studies.[128]

He served two years as District Attorney for Socorro and Sierra counties starting in 1905. He admitted serving in this capacity for two counties was straining.

As in most of his life, Elfego's position was viewed differently from the Anglo versus Hispanic perspective. When Baca became District Attorney for both Socorro and Sierra counties, the congressional committee working on statehood worried about his significant influence. However, the *Albuquerque Evening Citizen* admitted in 1906 that Baca "is making a vigorous and determined effort" to clean-up the counties and maintain the peace.

In the late 1890s, he invested and wrote a weekly column in a Spanish-language newspaper, *La Opinion Publica*. In 1907 he and other Hispanic journalists established *Alianza Hispana-American*. The goal of the alliance was to promote and familiarize Hispanics with the American constitutional process, as New Mexico strove toward statehood and other issues for *Nuevomexicanos*. Elfego later took ownership of *La Opinion Publica*.

Elfego worked with his friend, New Mexico's longtime Republican Senator Bronson Cutting, as a political investigator and promoted the maverick senator in the *La Opinion*. His journalistic career seems to support his legal and political career, which was still at the core of his life labors.

Francisquita and Elfego Baca approximately 1910. Photograph reproduction courtesy of the private collection of Gilbert Baca, Elfego Baca's grandnephew, Rio Rancho, New Mexico.

While continuing his law career during the early 1900s, Elfego along with Albuquerque attorney H. B. Fergusson argued Case 208 U.S. 515 Crary v. Dye to the United States Supreme Court, January 1908. The case concerned mining claims and was ruled in favor of Elfego's client.

Statehood for New Mexico was a long slow process, but New Mexico finally became a state in 1912. That same year, Elfego ran, unsuccessfully, for Congress as a Republican, in the new state of New Mexico. He remained in politics because of his ability to turn out the vote among the Hispanic population. During those years he worked as a private detective, and took a job as a bouncer in a casino across the border in Ciudad Juárez, Mexico. Elfego was hired as the United States Representative for Victoriano Huerta's government during the Mexican Revolution from 1913 to 1916.[129]

Elfego in uniform as an officer in the New Mexico National Guard around 1916. Photograph reproduction courtesy of the private collection of Gilbert Baca, Elfego Baca's grandnephew, Rio Rancho, New Mexico.

When Elfego was Sheriff of Socorro County in 1919, he used a unique method of arresting criminals who were indicted by the grand jury. He would send them a letter, telling them to come in and give themselves up, or he would come after them.

Warrants were made out and the deputies strained at the leash awaiting the orders of the big boss. Sheriff Baca was cool in the midst of his excited deputies:

"Calm yourselves," said Mr. Baca, "and send in the chief clerk."

The chief clerk entered. "Take that list of people wanted and send this letter to them," said Mr. Baca sitting back in his swivel chair and preparing for words.

"Dear Sir," dictated Elfego to the chief clerk.

"I have a warrant here for your arrest. Please come in by March 15 and give yourself up. If you don't I'll know that you intend to resist arrest, and I will feel justified in shooting you on sight when I come after you.

Yours truly, Elfego Baca, sheriff."[130]

They all came in except one and he answered the sheriff by letter. The man was Art Ford and this was his reply to the sheriff:

> "Ef yu want me, you blankety-blank Mexican, cum and git me. i will be under the big cottonwood by the river at noon on wednesday.
> Art Ford."[131]

On Wednesday, Elfego kept his appointment with great protest from his deputies. He waited, but Ford didn't show. When Elfego returned to his office, the not-so-brave Ford had given himself up and been put behind bars. Elfego used his reputation, of being invincible, to scare the criminals into giving themselves up.

Elfego Baca feared no man, however was a typical Spaniard; he respected women. Gilbert Baca, his grandnephew, recollected a family story:

> Around 1920 he was enforcing a new law which had to do with carrying firearms in town. He arrested Tomás Baca, his nephew and son of his older brother Abdenago. Tomás was carrying a pistol he picked up while fighting in World War I in Europe.
> Tomás' mother, Virginia Montoya de Baca, wife of Abdenago, got a call from her son, Tomás. Virginia wasted no time and hurried to the sheriff's office, where once there she demanded her son be let go. Elfego told her he had to enforce the law and it included members of the family. Virginia would have none of that and grabbed Elfego by the ear and twisted it until Elfego opened the cell door and Tomás was free.[132]

Gilbert Eugene Baca, Elfego Baca's grandnephew, 2015.

In 1920 Elfego ran unsuccessfully for a second term as District Attorney. He was fifty-five years old. He was described as a rather portly man with spectacles and a fire in his eyes. No doubt his varied career put some strain on his marriage to Francisquita and they formally divorced in 1922. However, she was living with Elfego at the family home in Albuquerque when he died in 1945.

Well into his later years, Elfego continued his public service. He was Jailer of Bernalillo County and ran for Governor in 1934 at the age of sixty-nine. In his final bid for public office, he ran for congress in 1940.

Congressional ribbon worn by Elfego Baca during his unsuccessful bid for congress in 1940. Photograph courtesy of the private collection of Gilbert Baca, Elfego Baca's grandnephew, Rio Rancho, New Mexico.

Elfego was never far from the law, on one side or the other. His reputation in the area was not over-rated. He lived a large life and was in most accounts larger-than-life. He was both respected and feared in the Socorro community. Starting in 1884, he never backed-down from a fight, never backed-down standing up for Hispanics, and feared no man:

> From then on I made up my mind, I wanted the outlaws to hear my steps a block away from me. I always had been for law and order and I will be until I die. Since that time I wanted to be an "A No-1" peace officer, likewise a criminal lawyer.[133]

Elfego's Spanish blood ran deep. He was an American, like all Americans with DNA from another place and time. He was hailed and he was jeered. Some accounts of his life treated his bravado as Post Traumatic Stress Disorder or PTSD and others wrote articles that made him look like a buffoon. The *Albuquerque Journal* consistently misspelled his first name, as *Elfigo*, when writing articles. In other writings, he has been dismissed only as a 'colorful character.' In reality, Elfego earned his life in the pit of the *jacal*, with a reputation to uphold for all the people. Elfego bested the Texas cowboys in battle and bested them in the courts. He carried on the fight for his state within the legal and political systems, understanding that he who controls the legal, political, and press wins. Elfego understood the American system and he worked it for the betterment of all Americans.

Elfego Baca passed away at his home in Albuquerque on August 27, 1945. He was eighty years old.

Conclusion

Throughout history, a single individual can make a difference. A single individual can stand up and change history. Elfego heard the call and was one of these rare individuals.

Cristóbal Colón headed across unchartered oceans and found the New World. Hernando Cortés, with the help of his faith, explored and conquered the Aztec empire. The leadership and courage of these two men paved the way for others to follow. One who followed was Juan de Vaca, ancestor of Elfego Baca.

Antonio Baca, son of Captain Cristóbal Baca and Ana Ortiz, gave his life for the Franciscan friars and his belief in the Catholic Church, rising up against a corrupt Governor Rosas in 1642. He was beheaded for his efforts.

A fifty-seven-year-old *Criollo* priest, Miguel Hidalgo y Costilla, went to war against Spain for the independence of Mexico and was killed, but his army of Indians and *mestizos* changed the caste system in Mexico and ultimately won Mexico's independence from Spain.

Epitacio Martinez stood alone and unarmed against rowdy Texas cowboys in a vain attempt to save *el Burro* from harm. For his effort, he was shot four times.

Talking about discrimination and injustice and standing tall against it are two different things. Talk is cheap. Bravery is expensive, maybe in blood. Like his Spanish ancestors, Elfego picked up his guns to answer the call. He did this for people he did not know. The DNA coursing through his bloodlines was more than enough courage. He had seen mob rule in Socorro. He had seen his brother lynched by vigilantes.

Elfego Baca, a lone man, stood up and fought back to stop the Texans from terrorizing the Hispanic villagers of the San Francisco valley. Elfego battled eighty Texas cowboys for thirty-six hours winning the battle, saying, "I will show the Texans there is at least one Mexican in the county who is not afraid of an American cowboy."

Elfego came from a long line of survivors. Survivors of the journey to the New World, famine, Indian battles, strife, disease and harsh living conditions, but survive they did and destiny prevailed. Elfego Baca lived!

Bibliography and Sources

This biography was written using published sources, both primary and secondary, with the exception of the interviews. This text notes the primary source(s) and by inference includes any secondary references. In cases where duplicate information was located in multiple sources, the author's primary source was referenced.

Books:

Baca, Elfego, *Here Comes Elfego! The Autobiography of Elfego Baca.* Albuquerque: The Vinegar Tom Press, 1924.

Ball, Larry D., *Elfego Baca in Life and Legend.* El Paso: Texas Western Press, 1992.

Ball, Larry D., *The United States Marshals of New Mexico and Arizona Territories 1846–1912.* Albuquerque: University of New Mexico Press, 1978.

Bryan, Howard, *Incredible Elfego Baca Good Man, Bad Man of the Old West.* Foreword by Rudolfo Anaya. Santa Fe: Clear Light Publishers, 1993.

Chávez, Fray Angélico, *Origins of New Mexico Families, A Genealogy of the Spanish Colonial Period Vol I.* Santa Fe: Historical Society of New Mexico, 1954.

Clarke, Mary Whatley, *The Slaughter Ranches & Their Makers.* Austin: Jenkins Publishing Co., 1979.

Collinson, Frank, *Life in the Saddle.* Norman: University of Oklahoma Press, 1963.

Cook, James H., *Fifty Years on the Old Frontier.* Norman: University of Oklahoma Press, 1923.

Crichton, Kyle Samuel, *Law and Order, Ltd. The Rousing Life of Elfego Baca of New Mexico.* New Edition, Santa Fe: Sunstone Press, 2008.

French, Captain William, *Some Recollections of a Western Ranchman.* New York: Frederick A. Stokes, 1928.

García, Genaro, *The True History of the Conquest of New Spain*, from the original Manuscript by Bernal Díaz del Castillo, translated by Alfred Percival. Maudslay. London: Printed for the Hakluyt Society, 1908.

Gillett, James B., *Six Years with the Texas Rangers 1875–1881.* New Haven: Yale University Press, 1925.

Hammond, George P., *Don Juan de Oñate and the Founding of New Mexico.* Santa Fe: El Palacio Press, 1927.

L'Aloge, Bob, *The Incident of New Mexico's Nightriders, A True Account of the Socorro Vigilantes.* Foreword by Howard Bryan. Sunnyside: Brand Books, 1992.

Linares, Fernando Orozco, *Historia de México*, de la época Prehispánica a nuestros días. Mexico: Panorama Editorial, S.A., 1982.

McGeagh, Robert, *Juan de Oñate's Colony in the Wilderness*. Santa Fe: Sunstone Press, 1990.

Nieto-Phillips, John M., *The Language of Blood, The Making of Spanish-American Identity in New Mexico, 1880s–1930s*. Albuquerque: University of New Mexico Press, 2004.

Payne, Viola M., *Three Angels Over Rancho Grande*. Mountain View: Pacific Press Publishing Association, 1975.

Prince, La Baron Bradford, *New Mexico's Struggle for Statehood*. New Edition, Santa Fe: Sunstone Press, 2010.

Read, Benjamin M.,*Guerra Mexico-Americana*. Santa Fe: Compania impresora del Nuevo Mexicano, 1910.

Sager, Stan, *¡Viva Elfego! The Case for Elfego Baca, Hispanic Hero*. Santa Fe: Sunstone Press, 2008.

Seitz, Don C., *From Kaw Teepee To Capitol, The Life of Charles Curtis, Indian, Who Has Risen to High Estate*. New York: Fredrick A. Stokes Company, 1928.

Simmons, Marc, *The Last Conquistador, Juan de Oñate and the Settling of the Far Southwest*. Norman: University of Oklahoma Press, 1991.

Yoakum, Henderson K., *History of Texas from Its First Settlement in 1685 to Its Annexation by the United States in 1846, Volume 1*. New York: Redfield, 1856.

Articles:

H. Allen Anderson, "Slaughter, William Baxter," Handbook of Texas Online, Texas State Historical Association.
www.tshaonline.org/handbook/online/articles/fsl14

Hernando Cortes, "Second Letter of Hernando Cortés to Charles V," Early Americas Digital Archive.
http://mith.umd.edu/eada/html/display.php?docs=cortez_letter2.xml

Robert Eveleth and Paul Harden, "Socorro's Territorial Saloons," El Defensor Chieftain Newspaper, Saturday, October 2, 2010.
www.caminorealheritage.org/PH/y1010_saloons_1.pdf

Elisa Figueroa, Omar Guerrero, Julie Williams, Jeremiah Tovar and Rene Ochoa, "James Gillett Showed Courage in El Paso," Borderlands 23 (2004-2005): 4, 10 .Borderlands. EPCC Libraries.
http://dnn.epcc.edu/nwlibrary/borderlands

Richard Flint and Shirley Cushing, "Bernardo López de Mendizábal," New Mexico Office of the State Historian. www.newmexicohistory.org/filedetails.php?fileID=480

Richard Flint and Shirley Cushing, "Diego de Vargas (1644-1704)," New Mexico Office of the State Historian. www.newmexicohistory.org/filedetails.php?fileID=482#

David Gonzales and Jonathan A. Ortega, "Onofre Baca – Socorro Lynching victim and his brother Elfego Baca – an American Legend," Herencia Journal Volume 3 Issue 1, January 1995

Paul Harden, "The Mayors of Socorro," El Defensor Chieftain Newspaper, www.dchieftain.com/2010/04/03/the-mayors-of-socorro

Claudia Hazlewood, "Slaughter, George Webb," Handbook of Texas Online, Texas State Historical Association. www.tshaonline.org/handbook/online/articles/fsl02

Margaret Swett Henson, "Anglo-American Colonization," Handbook of Texas Online, Texas State Historical Association. www.tshaonline.org/handbook/online/articles/uma01

Gerald F. Kozlowski, "Onate, Juan de," Handbook of Texas Online, Texas State Historical Association.

www.tshaonline.org/handbook/online/articles/fon02

Medieval Sourcebook, "Christopher Columbus Journal," Hanover College. http://history.hanover.edu/courses/excerpts/111columbus.html

Doris Meyer, "Benjamin Read New Mexico Historian," The New Mexico Office of the State Historian, State Records Center and Archives. www.newmexicohistory.org/filedetails_docs.php?fileID=21924

Charles Montgomery, "Becoming Spanish-American: Race and Rhetoric in New Mexico Politics 1880-1928," Journal of American Ethnic History, Vol. 20, No. 4, Summer, 2001, University of Illinois Press. www.jstor.org/discover/10.2307/27502746?uid=3739552&uid=2129&uid=2&uid=70&uid=4&uid=3739256&sid=47698858090387

National Humanities Center, "Letters Home: Correspondence from Spanish colonists in Mexico City and Puebla to relatives in Spain, 1558-1589," http://nationalhumanitiescenter.org/pds/amerbegin/permanence/text1/LettersSpanish.pdf

A. H Sevier, and Nathan Clifford and Luis de la Rosa, "Treaty with Mexico (February 2, 1848)," www.mexica.net/guadhida.php

SparkNotes Editors, "SparkNote on Westward Expansion (1807-1912)," SparkNotes LLC. n.d.

www.sparknotes.com/history/american/westwardexpansion/section7.rhtml

Janet Smith, "Interview with Elfego Baca, " Library of Congress, 7-13-1936

Andy Stiney, "How a New Mexico Find Revolutionized Archaeology," New West, 3-29-2011, www.newwest.net/topic/article/how_a_new_mexico_find_revolutionized_archaeology/C41/L41/

Robert J. Torrez, "New Mexico and the Mexican American War," New Mexico office of the State Historian. www.newmexicohistory.org/filedetails.php?fileID=21394#

William H. Wroth, "Armijo, Manuel," New Mexico Office of the State Historian. www.newmexicohistory.org/filedetails.php?fileID=549#

Aminta Cavazos Zarate, "Spanish and Mexican Land Grants in Texas," http://e-genealogylinks.com

David Zax, "Ancient Citadel," Travel. Smithsonian Magazine, May 2008. www.smithsonianmag.com/travel/da-ancient-citadel.html

Special Collections:

Special Collections Department, Zimmerman Library, Center for Southwest Research, University of New Mexico, Elfego Baca Collections, Albuquerque, New Mexico

U.S. Department of Commerce, Bureau of the Census, as provided through www.ancestry.com

    1860 Census, Socorro County, New Mexico. www.censusrecords.com
    1870 Census, Socorro County, New Mexico. www.censusrecords.com
    1880 Census, Socorro County, New Mexico. www.censusrecords.com

Websites (as of October, 2012):

http://aces.nmsu.edu/pubs/resourcesmag/spring98/3000years.html

http://en.wikipedia.org; Text is available under the Creative Commons Attribution-ShareAlike License. Wikipedia® is a registered trademark of the Wikimedia Foundation, Inc., a non-profit organization:

> http://en.wikipedia.org/wiki/Acoma_Massacre
> http://en.wikipedia.org/wiki/Alvar_Cabeza_de_Vaca
> http://en.wikipedia.org/wiki/Antonio_L%C3%B3pez_de_Santa_Anna
> http://en.wikipedia.org/wiki/Battle_of_San_Jacinto
> http://en.wikipedia.org/wiki/Criollo_people
> http://en.wikipedia.org/wiki/Elfego_Baca
> http://en.wikipedia.org/wiki/El_Morro_National_Monument
> http://en.wikipedia.org/wiki/Ferdinand_II_of_Aragon
> http://en.wikipedia.org/wiki/Francisco_Coronado
> http://en.wikipedia.org/wiki/Francisco_V%C3%A1squez_de_Coronado
> http://en.wikipedia.org/wiki/Frisco_Shootout
> http://en.wikipedia.org/wiki/Gunfighters
> http://en.wikipedia.org/wiki/Gunfight_at_the_O.K._Corral
> http://en.wikipedia.org/wiki/Hern%C3%A1n_Cort%C3%A9s

http://en.wikipedia.org/wiki/Homestead_Act
http://en.wikipedia.org/wiki/James_B._Gillett
http://en.wikipedia.org/wiki/James_Polk
http://en.wikipedia.org/wiki/John_L._O%27Sullivan
http://en.wikipedia.org/wiki/Juan_de_O%C3%B1ate
http://en.wikipedia.org/wiki/List_of_Old_West_gunfights
http://en.wikipedia.org/wiki/List_of_Western_lawmen
http://en.wikipedia.org/wiki/Mestizo
http://en.wikipedia.org/wiki/Miguel_Hidalgo_y_Costilla
http://en.wikipedia.org/wiki/Moses_Austin
http://en.wikipedia.org/wiki/Native_American_name_controversy
http://en.wikipedia.org/wiki/Narv%C3%A1ez_expedition
http://en.wikipedia.org/wiki/Peninsulars
http://en.wikipedia.org/wiki/Sam_Houston
http://en.wikipedia.org/wiki/Texas_annexation
http://en.wikipedia.org/wiki/Wild_Bill_Hickok_%E2%80%93_Davis_Tutt_shootout

http://chroniclingamerica.loc.gov

http://dig.lib.niu.edu/mexicanwar/origins.html

http://infinito9.com/landgrants/history.html

http://k12west.mrdonn.org/ColonialMexico.html

http://nationalhumanitiescenter.org/pds/amerbegin/permanence/text1/LettersSpanish.pdf

http://newmexicowanderings.com/socorro3.htm

http://nmmagazine.com/history.php

http://wc.rootsweb.ancestry.com

www.ancestry.com

www apstudynotes.org/us-history/topics/cattle-frontiers-and-farming/

www.city-data.com/states/Texas-History.html

www.legendsofamerica.com/we-gunfighterindex-c-d.html

www.legendsofamerica.com/we-gunfights3.html#O.K.%20Corral%20Gunfight%20%281881%29

www.legendsofamerica.com/we-elfegobaca.html

www.lib.utexas.edu/maps

www.mexconnect.com/articles/291-miguel-hidalgo-the-father-who-fathered-a-country-1753%E2%80%931811

www.newmexicohistory.org/filedetails.php?fileID=480

www.newwest.net/topic/article/how_a_new_mexico_find_revolutionized_archaeology/C41/L41/

www.nps.gov/elmo/historyculture/the-spaniards.htm

www.sparknotes.com/history/american/westwardexpansion/section7.rhtml

www.sunofmexico.com/mexican_people.php

www.tshaonline.org/handbook/online/articles/jcc01

www.tshaonline.org/handbook/online/articles/uma01

Interviews:

Interviews with Gilbert Eugene Baca, Elfego Baca's grandnephew

Interviews with Henry Martinez, Epitacio Martinez's great-grandson

Notes

[1] http://en. wikipedia.org/wiki/Frisco_Shootout

[2] Translation Christopher Columbus Journal," (http://history.hanover.edu/courses/excerpts/111columbus.html)

[3] García, *The True History of the Conquest of New Spain*, P 139

[4] Cortés, "Second Letter of Hernando Cortés to Charles V," 1520, P 23-24

[5] http://nmmagazine.com/history.php

[6] Kozlowski,"Onate, Juan de," Handbook of Texas Online, (www.tshaonline.org/handbook/online/articles/fon02)

[7] Hammond, *Juan de Oñate and the Founding of New Mexico*, P 19-20

[8] Hammond, *Juan de Oñate and the Founding of New Mexico*, P 19-20

[9] Hammond, *Juan de Oñate and the Founding of New Mexico*, P 90-91

[10] Hammond, *Juan de Oñate and the Founding of New Mexico*, P 102-103

[11] Hammond, *Juan de Oñate and the Founding of New Mexico*, P 116-117

[12] http://en.wikipedia.org/wiki/Acoma_Massacre

[13] Chávez, *Origins of New Mexico Families, A Genealogy of the Spanish Colonial Period*, P 9

[14] www.nps.gov/elmo/historyculture/the-spaniards.htm

[15] Flint and Cushing, "Diego de Vargas (1644-1704)," (www.newmexicohistory.org/filedetails.php?fileID=482#)

[16] Linares, *Historia de México*, translation by author, P 195

[17] SparkNotes Editors, "SparkNote on Westward Expansion (1807–1912),"

(www.sparknotes.com/history/american/westwardexpansion/section7.rhtml)

[18] Henson, "Anglo-American Colonization," Handbook of Texas Online (www.tshaonline.org/handbook/online/articles/uma01)

[19] Yoakum, *History of Texas from Its First Settlement in 1685 to Its Annexation by the United States in 1846*, Volume 1, P 307

[20] Yoakum, *History of Texas from Its First Settlement in 1685 to Its Annexation by the United States in 1846*, Volume 1 Appendix No. VI, P 465

[21] http://city-data.com/states/Texas-History.html

[22] Hazlewood, "Slaughter, George Webb," Handbook of Texas Online (www.tshaonline.org/handbook/online/articles/fsl02)

[23] Linares, *Historia de México*, translation by author, P 196-197

[24] Yoakum, *History of Texas from Its First Settlement in 1685 to Its Annexation by the United States in 1846*, Volume 1 Appendix No. VI, P 365-366

[25] Wroth, "Armijo, Manuel," (www.newmexicohistory.org/filedetails.php?fileID=549#)

[26] Torrez, "New Mexico and the Mexican American War," (www.newmexicohistory.org/filedetails.php?fileID=21394#)

[27] Torrez, "New Mexico and the Mexican American War," (www.newmexicohistory.org/filedetails.php?fileID=21394#)

[28] Meyer, "Benjamin Read New Mexico Historian," (www.newmexicohistory.org/filedetails_docs.php?fileID=21924)

[29] Nieto-Phillips, *The Language of Blood, The Making of Spanish-American Identity in New Mexico, 1880s–1930s*, P 69

[30] Prince, *New Mexico's Struggle for Statehood*, P 62-63
[31] Payne, *Three Angels Over Rancho Grande*, P 11
[32] Payne, *Three Angels Over Rancho Grande*, P 11-13
[33] Payne, *Three Angels Over Rancho Grande*, P 15
[34] Payne, *Three Angels Over Rancho Grande*, P 30
[35] French, *Some Recollections of a Western Ranchman*, P 42-43
[36] www. apstudynotes.org/us-history/topics/cattle-frontiers-and-farming/
[37] Clarke, *The Slaughter Ranches and Their Makers*, P 19
[38] Clarke, *The Slaughter Ranches and Their Makers*, P 167
[39] Chávez, *Origins of New Mexico Families, A Genealogy of the Spanish Colonial Period*, P 9
[40] Mc Geagh, *Juan de Oñate's Colony in the Wilderness*, P 38
[41] Simmons, *The Last Conquistador, Juan de Oñate and the Settling of the Far Southwest*, P 158
[42] Simmons, *The Last Conquistador, Juan de Oñate and the Settling of the Far Southwest*, P 158
[43] Chávez, *Origins of New Mexico Families, A Genealogy of the Spanish Colonial Period*, P 10
[44] Flint and Cushing, "Bernardo López de Mendizábal," (www.newmexicohistory.org/filedetails.php?fileID=480)
[45] Chávez, *Origins of New Mexico Families, A Genealogy of the Spanish Colonial Period*, P 10
[46] http://wc.rootsweb.ancestry.com/
[47] Ball, *Elfego Baca in Life and Legend*, P 1-2
[48] Crichton, *Law and Order, Ltd. The Rousing Life of Elfego Baca of New Mexico*, P 6
[49] Sager, *¡Viva Elfego! The Case for Elfego Baca, Hispanic Hero*, P 11; Ball, *Elfego Baca in Life and Legend*, P 3; Bryan,

Incredible Elfego Baca Good Man, Bad Man of the Old West, P 9

[50] Baca, *Here Comes Elfego!, The Autobiography of Elfego Baca*, P 10-11

[51] Baca, *Here Comes Elfego!, The Autobiography of Elfego Baca*, P 11-12

[52] Baca, *Here Comes Elfego!, The Autobiography of Elfego Baca*, P 13-14

[53] Baca, *Here Comes Elfego!, The Autobiography of Elfego Baca*, P 11

[54] L'Aloge, *The Incident of New Mexico's Nightriders, A True Account of the Socorro Vigilantes*, P 34-35

[55] Montgomery, "Becoming 'Spanish-American': Race and Rhetoric in New Mexico Politics, 1880-1928"

[56] Interview with Gilbert Baca, grandnephew of Elfego Baca, 2012

[57] L'Aloge, *The Incident of New Mexico's Nightriders, A True Account of the Socorro Vigilantes*, P 32

[58] http://wc.rootsweb.ancestry.com/cgi-bin/igm.cgi?op=GET&db=c_bacaslater&id=I359

[59] L'Aloge, *The Incident of New Mexico's Nightriders, A True Account of the Socorro Vigilantes*, P 35-38

[60] Gonzales and Ortega, "Onofre Baca – Socorro Lynching victim and his brother Elfego Baca – an American legend"

[61] L'Aloge, *The Incident of New Mexico's Nightriders, A True Account of the Socorro Vigilantes*, P 42

[62] L'Aloge, *The Incident of New Mexico's Nightriders, A True Account of the Socorro Vigilantes*, P 42

[63] Gonzales and Ortega, "Onofre Baca – Socorro Lynching victim and his brother Elfego Baca – an American legend"

[64] Figueroa, et al, "James Gillett Showed Courage in El Paso," (http://dnn.epcc.edu/nwlibrary/borderlands)

[65] Gillett, *Six Years with the Texas Rangers 1875–1881*, P 217-218

[66] L'Aloge, *The Incident of New Mexico's Nightriders, A True Account of the Socorro Vigilantes*, P 109-120

[67] Gillett, *Six Years with the Texas Rangers 1875–1881*, P 222-224

[68] Gonzales and Ortega, "Onofre Baca – Socorro Lynching victim and his brother Elfego Baca – an American legend"

[69] Crichton, *Law and Order, Ltd. The Rousing Life of Elfego Baca of New Mexico*, P 8-9

[70] Crichton, *Law and Order, Ltd. The Rousing Life of Elfego Baca of New Mexico*, P 10-13

[71] Eveleth and Harden, "Socorro's Territorial Saloons," El Defensor Chieftain, (www.caminorealheritage.org/PH/y1010_saloons_1.pdf)

[72] Smith, *Interview with Elfego Baca*, Works Project Administration interview

[73] Collinson, *Life in the Saddle*, P 218

[74] Ball, *The United States Marshals of New Mexico and Arizona Territories 1846-1912*, P 81

[75] Baca, *Here Comes Elfego!, The Autobiography of Elfego Baca*, P 15-16

[76] Simmons, *The Last Conquistador, Juan de Oñate and the Settling of the Far Southwest*, P 20

[77] Interview with Gilbert Baca, grandnephew of Elfego Baca, 2012

[78] Payne, *Three Angels Over Rancho Grande*, P 31-32

[79] Crichton, *Law and Order, Ltd. The Rousing Life of Elfego Baca of New Mexico*, P 28

[80] Crichton, *Law and Order, Ltd. The Rousing Life of Elfego Baca of New Mexico*, P 30

[81] Crichton, *Law and Order, Ltd. The Rousing Life of Elfego Baca of New Mexico*, P 29-30

[82] Baca, *Here Comes Elfego!, The Autobiography of Elfego Baca*, P 18

[83] Cook, *Fifty Years on the Old Frontier*, P 223

[84] French, *Some Recollections of a Western Ranchman*, P 44

[85] French, *Some Recollections of a Western Ranchman*, P 43

[86] Baca, *Here Comes Elfego!, The Autobiography of Elfego Baca*, P 18

[87] Baca, *Here Comes Elfego!, The Autobiography of Elfego Baca*, P 18

[88] Cook, *Fifty Years on the Old Frontier*, P 221

[89] French, *Some Recollections of a Western Ranchman*, P 42

[90] Cook, *Fifty Years on the Old Frontier*, P 222

[91] French, *Some Recollections of a Western Ranchman*, P 44

[92] Cook, *Fifty Years on the Old Frontier*, P 224

[93] Baca, *Here Comes Elfego!, The Autobiography of Elfego Baca*, P 18-19

[94] Cook, *Fifty Years on the Old Frontier*, P 223-224

[95] Crichton, *Law and Order, Ltd. The Rousing Life of Elfego Baca of New Mexico*, P 33

[96] Baca, *Here Comes Elfego!, The Autobiography of Elfego Baca*, P 19

[97] Baca, *Here Comes Elfego!, The Autobiography of Elfego Baca*, P 20

[98] Crichton, *Law and Order, Ltd. The Rousing Life of Elfego Baca of New Mexico*, P 34

[99] Crichton, *Law and Order, Ltd. The Rousing Life of Elfego Baca of New Mexico*, P 34

[100] French, *Some Recollections of a Western Ranchman*, P 46-47

[101] Cook, *Fifty Years on the Old Frontier*, P 224-225

[102] French, *Some Recollections of a Western Ranchman*, P 47

[103] French, *Some Recollections of a Western Ranchman*, P 47

[104] French, *Some Recollections of a Western Ranchman*, P 47

[105] Crichton, *Law and Order, Ltd. The Rousing Life of Elfego Baca of New Mexico*, P 36

[106] French, *Some Recollections of a Western Ranchman*, P 48

[107] French, *Some Recollections of a Western Ranchman*, P 48-49

[108] Baca, *Here Comes Elfego!, The Autobiography of Elfego Baca*, P 20

[109] Cook, *Fifty Years on the Old Frontier*, P 225; *Law and Order, Ltd.*, P 41

[110] Crichton, *Law and Order, Ltd. The Rousing Life of Elfego Baca of New Mexico*, P 37-38

[111] Crichton, *Law and Order, Ltd. The Rousing Life of Elfego Baca of New Mexico*, P 39

[112] Crichton, *Law and Order, Ltd. The Rousing Life of Elfego Baca of New Mexico*, P 39-40

[113] Payne, *Three Angels Over Rancho Grande*, P 302

[114] French, *Some Recollections of a Western Ranchman*, P 51

[115] Crichton, *Law and Order, Ltd. The Rousing Life of Elfego Baca of New Mexico*, P 43

[116] Crichton, *Law and Order, Ltd. The Rousing Life of Elfego Baca of New Mexico*, P 43

[117] Baca, *Here Comes Elfego!, The Autobiography of Elfego Baca*, P 21

[118] Cook, *Fifty Years on the Old Frontier*, P 226-227

[119] Crichton, *Law and Order, Ltd. The Rousing Life of Elfego Baca of New Mexico*, P 45-46

[120] Baca, *Here Comes Elfego!, The Autobiography of Elfego Baca*, P 21

[121] French, *Some Recollections of a Western Ranchman*, P 42-43

[122] Nieto-Phillips, *The Language of Blood, The Making of Spanish-American Identity in New Mexico, 1880s–1930s*, P 115

[123] French, *Some Recollections of a Western Ranchman*, P 53

[124] Sager, *¡Viva Elfego! The Case for Elfego Baca, Hispanic Hero*, P 51

[125] Bryan, *Incredible Elfego Baca Good Man, Bad Man of the Old West*, P 47

[126] Ball, *Elfego Baca in Life and Legend*, P 41

[127] Harden, "The Mayors of Socorro," (www.dchieftain.com/2010/04/03/the-mayors-of-socorro)

[128] Baca, *Here Comes Elfego!, The Autobiography of Elfego Baca*, P 5

[129] Crichton, *Law and Order, Ltd. The Rousing Life of Elfego Baca of New Mexico*, P 130-131

[130] Crichton, *Law and Order, Ltd. The Rousing Life of Elfego Baca of New Mexico*, P 83-85

[131] Crichton, *Law and Order, Ltd. The Rousing Life of Elfego Baca of New Mexico*, P 85

[132] Interview with Gilbert Baca, grandnephew of Elfego Baca, 2012

[133] Baca, *Here Comes Elfego!, The Autobiography of Elfego Baca*, P 22

www.ingramcontent.com/pod-product-compliance
Lightning Source LLC
Chambersburg PA
CBHW070847050426
42453CB00012B/2081